DISCARD

HISTORY OF EAST AFRICA

THE DIAGRAM GROUP

Facts On File, Inc.

History of Africa: History of East Africa
Copyright © 2003 by The Diagram Group

Diagram Visual Information Ltd

Editorial director:	Denis Kennedy
Editor:	Peter Harrison
Contributor:	Simon Adams
Consultant:	Keith Lye
Indexer:	Martin Hargreaves
Senior designer:	Lee Lawrence
Designers:	Claire Bojczuk, Christian Owens
Illustrators:	Kathy McDougall, Graham Rosewarne
Research:	Neil McKenna, Patricia Robertson

Library of Congress Cataloging-in-Publication Data
History of East Africa / the Diagram Group.
    p. cm. – (History of Africa)
  Includes bibliographical references and index.
  ISBN 0-8160-5060-0 (set) – ISBN 0-8160-5063-5
  1. Africa, Eastern–History–Miscellanea. I. Diagram Group. II. Series.

DT365.5 .H47 2003
967.6'03–dc21   2002035204

Facts On File books are available at special discounts when purchased in bulk quantities for businesses, associations, institutions, or sales promotions. Please call our Special Sales Department in New York at 212/967-8800 or 800/322-8755.

You can find Facts On File on the World Wide Web at: http://www.factsonfile.com

Printed in the United States of America

EB DIAG 10 9 8 7 6 5 4 3 2 1

Contents

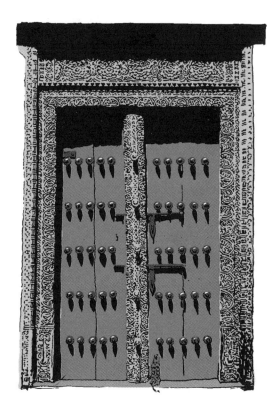

FOREWORD

The six-volume History of Africa series has been designed as a companion set to the Peoples of Africa series. Although, of necessity, there is some overlap between the two series, there is also a significant shift in focus. Whereas Peoples of Africa focuses on ethnographic issues, that is the the individual human societies which make up the continent, History of Africa graphically presents a historical overview of the political forces that shaped the vast continent today.

History of East Africa starts off with a description of the region in depth, including its religions, land, climate, and the languages spoken there today, with particular relevance to the colonial legacy as it affected the spoken word region-by-region. There follows an overview of events from prehistory to the present day, and a brief discussion of the historical sources that help us to learn about the past.

The major part of the book comprises an in-depth examination of the history of the region from the first humans through the early civilizations or chiefdoms; the development of trade with other countries; the arrival of European colonists, and the effect this had on the indigenous peoples; the struggles for independence in the last century; and the current political situation in the nation, or island states, in the new millennium.

Interspersed throughout the main text of the book are special features on a variety of topics which bring the region to life, such as the rock churches of Lalibela, Swahili culture and history, the Kikuyu, the Mau Mau rebellion in Kenya, and the impact of tourism in East Africa today.

Throughout the book the reader will also find timelines which list major events combined with maps, diagrams, and illustrations, presented in two-color form throughout, which help to explain these events in more detail, and place them within the context of world events. Finally, there is a glossary which defines unfamiliar words used in the book, and a comprehensive index. Taken together with the other five volumes in this series, *History of East Africa* will provide the reader with a memorable snapshot of Africa as a continent with a rich history.

Dates

In this book we use the dating system BCE – Before Common Era – and CE – Common Era. 1 CE is the same year as 1 AD. We have used this system to cater for different religions and beliefs which do not recognize a Christian-based dating system.

The religions of East Africa

The vast majority of people in East Africa are either Muslim or Christian. Arab traders who settled on the coast introduced Islam into the region about 1,000 years ago. It did not spread much beyond the coastal regions until the 19th century. Ethiopia has a long history of Christianity extending back more than 1,600 years. European missionaries introduced Christianity to other parts of East Africa in the 19th century. East African Asians follow the beliefs of the subcontinent – Hinduism, Islam, Sikhism, Christianity, and Zoroastrianism – while the Falasha of Ethiopia are Jews.

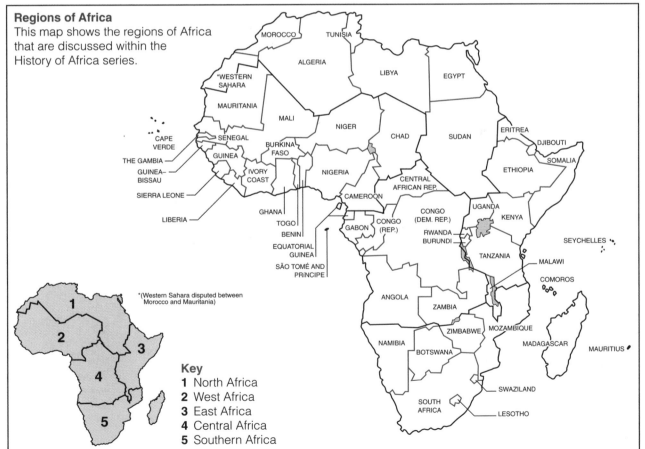

Regions of Africa
This map shows the regions of Africa that are discussed within the History of Africa series.

*(Western Sahara disputed between Morocco and Mauritania)

Key
1 North Africa
2 West Africa
3 East Africa
4 Central Africa
5 Southern Africa

© DIAGRAM

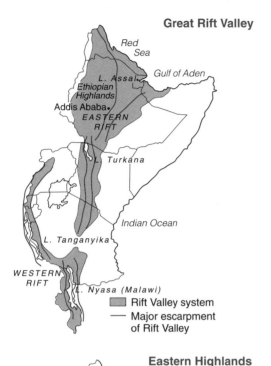

Great Rift Valley

Red Sea
Gulf of Aden
L. Assal
Ethiopian Highlands
Addis Ababa
EASTERN RIFT
L. Turkana
Indian Ocean
L. Tanganyika
WESTERN RIFT
L. Nyasa (Malawi)

■ Rift Valley system
— Major escarpment of Rift Valley

Land

East Africa consists of 11 countries: Burundi, Djibouti, Eritrea, Ethiopia, Kenya, Malawi, Rwanda, Somalia, Tanzania, and Uganda, as well as the Indian Ocean island nation of the Seychelles. It is bordered on the north by the Red Sea and the Gulf of Aden, and on the east by the Indian Ocean. It is Africa's most mountainous area and it contains the southern section of the Great Rift Valley, a depression that extends from the Jordan River valley in southwest Asia south through East Africa. Much of the region consists of plateaus, in places overlooked by snowcapped peaks, and gashed by steep troughs hundreds of miles long. Offshore islands dot the southern coastline.

East Africa has the continent's highest point – Mount Kilimanjaro at 19, 340 ft (5,895 m) – and its lowest point – 509 ft (155 m) below sea level at Lake Assal, Djibouti. Africa's highest city is the Ethiopian capital, Addis Ababa, 8,000 ft (2,400 m) above sea level. From lakes Victoria, Edward, and Tana flows the Nile, the world's longest river at 4,160 miles (6,695 km). The most densely populated areas of East Africa include much of Malawi, Rwanda, Burundi, Uganda, southern Kenya, and the Ethiopian uplands.

Eastern Highlands

Red Sea
Gulf of Aden
L. Victoria
Indian Ocean

■ Eastern Highlands

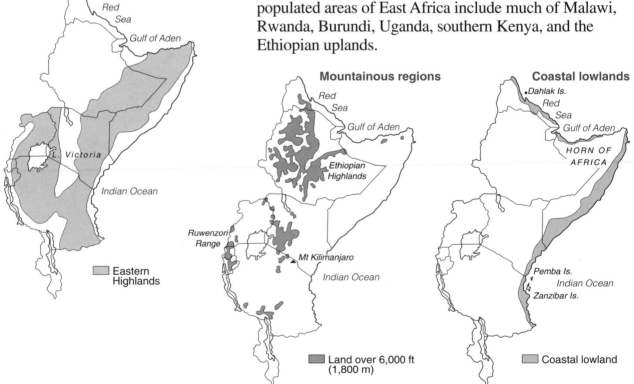

Mountainous regions

Red Sea
Gulf of Aden
Ethiopian Highlands
Ruwenzori Range
Mt Kilimanjaro
Indian Ocean

■ Land over 6,000 ft (1,800 m)

Coastal lowlands

Dahlak Is.
Red Sea
Gulf of Aden
HORN OF AFRICA
Pemba Is.
Indian Ocean
Zanzibar Is.

■ Coastal lowland

Climate

East Africa has a variety of climates. Many areas have fairly constant daily temperatures, ranging from hot to cold depending on the altitude. The Horn of Africa – Somalia and neighboring parts of Ethiopia and Djibouti – the Red Sea coast, and northeast Kenya have an arid to semiarid climate, largely hot and dry but with great swings in daily temperature. Apart from the highlands of Ethiopia and the Great Rift Valley, the rest of East Africa has a hot, tropical climate with both wet and dry seasons, although some western areas close to the equator receive several inches of rain every month. The highlands generally have cooler and wetter climates than elsewhere.

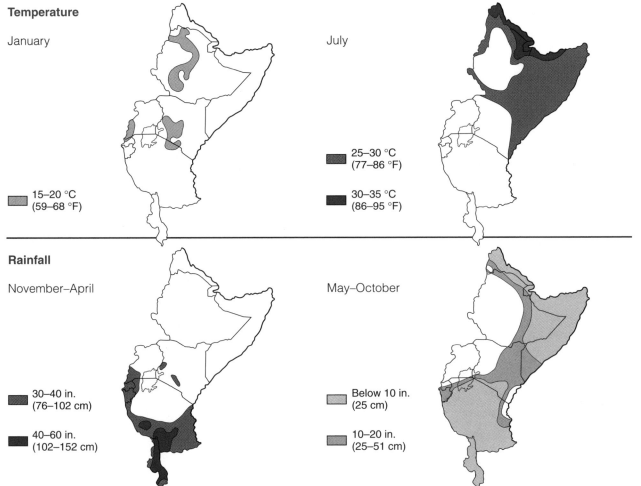

Temperature

January

July

15–20 °C
(59–68 °F)

25–30 °C
(77–86 °F)

30–35 °C
(86–95 °F)

Rainfall

November–April

May–October

30–40 in.
(76–102 cm)

40–60 in.
(102–152 cm)

Below 10 in.
(25 cm)

10–20 in.
(25–51 cm)

© DIAGRAM

7

Pierre Buyoya,
president of Burundi
in 1987 and 1996

Issias Afewerki, first
president of Eritrea
in May, 1993

Daniel arap Moi,
president of Kenya from
1978–2002

Paul Kagame,
president of Rwanda
in 2000

Mohamed Ibrahim Egal,
president of Somaliland
Republic in 1990s

Apollo Milton Obote,
first prime minister of
Uganda in 1962

Ismail Omar Guelleh,
president of Djibouti
in April,1999

Haile-Mariam
Mengistu, first
president of Ethiopia
1974–1991

Bakili Muluzi,
president of Malawi
in 1994 and 1999

James Mancham,
prime minister of the
Seychelles in 1970.

Ali Hassan Mwinyi,
president of
Tanzania in 1985
and 1990

Burundi
Burundi became independent in 1962 but, since then, it has been wracked by conflict between its majority Hutu and minority Tutsi peoples. The population are mostly Roman Catholic.

Djibouti
Djibouti is the second smallest country in the region. The population comprises the southern Issa, and the northern Afar peoples, both of whom are Muslim.

Eritrea
The Tigre, or Tigrinya, is the largest of the nine major ethnic groups in Eritrea. The population is half Muslim, half Christian.

Ethiopia
Ethiopia is the biggest and most populous country in the region, its people comprising 76 different ethnic groups. After years of dictatorial rule, it is now a multiparty federal state.

Kenya
Kenya is the fourth largest country in the region with a population made up of 70 different ethnic groups. The majority of the population are Christian, although one quarter follows traditional beliefs; six percent are Muslim.

Malawi
Half the population of Malawi is Christian, 20 percent is Muslim, while the rest of the people follow traditional beliefs.

Rwanda
Rwanda has been riven by ethnic conflict between its minority Tutsi and majority Hutu peoples. The majority of the people are Roman Catholics and live in just 10,165 square miles, making Rwanda the most densely populated country in the region.

Seychelles
Seychelles has the smallest population in East Africa, the vast majority of whom are Roman Catholic Creoles (mixed Africans and Europeans).

Somalia
Since gaining independence in 1961, military coups and civil war have torn the country apart. The population is overwhelmingly Sunni Muslim, and Somali, further divided into clans.

Tanzania
The population, the second biggest in the region, includes 120 ethnic Bantu-speaking groups and is one-third Christian, one-third Muslim, and one-third traditional believers.

Uganda
Decades of dictatorial rule and ethnic strife have impoverished the country. Its population comprises 13 main ethnic groups, the majority of whom are Christians.

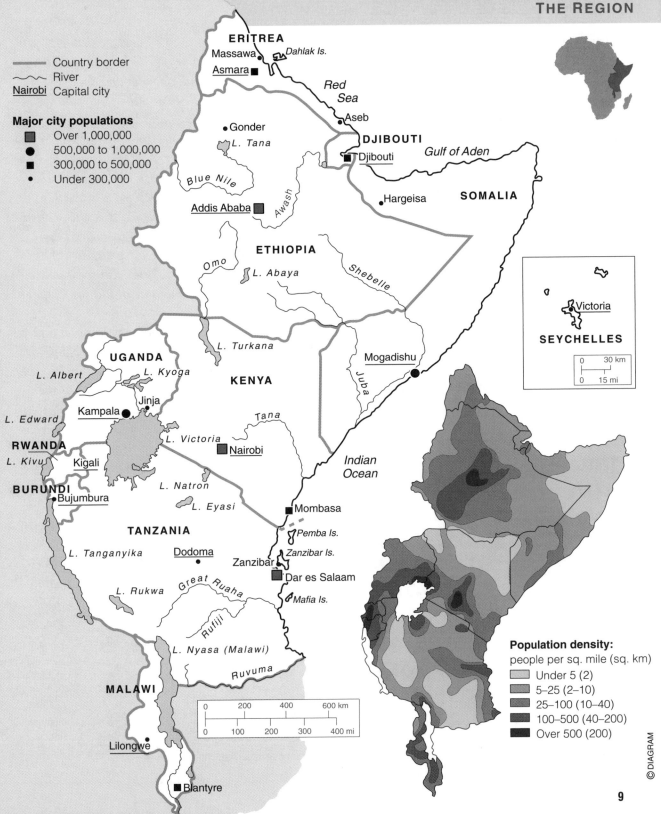

ERITREA
Massawa
Dahlak Is.
Asmara ■
Red Sea
Aseb
Gonder •
L. Tana
DJIBOUTI
Djibouti ■
Gulf of Aden
Addis Ababa ■
Awash
Hargeisa •
SOMALIA
ETHIOPIA
Omo
L. Abaya
Shebelle

Country border
River
Nairobi Capital city

Major city populations
■ Over 1,000,000
● 500,000 to 1,000,000
■ 300,000 to 500,000
• Under 300,000

UGANDA
L. Albert
L. Kyoga
Kampala ● Jinja
L. Edward
RWANDA
L. Kivu
Kigali
BURUNDI
Bujumbura •
TANZANIA
L. Tanganyika
L. Natron
L. Eyasi
Dodoma
L. Rukwa
Great Ruaha
L. Victoria
Nairobi ■
Tana
KENYA
L. Turkana
Juba
Mogadishu ●
Indian Ocean
Mombasa ■
Pemba Is.
Zanzibar *Zanzibar Is.*
Dar es Salaam ■
Mafia Is.
Rufiji
L. Nyasa (Malawi)
Ruvuma
MALAWI
Lilongwe ●
Blantyre ■

Victoria
SEYCHELLES
0 30 km
0 15 mi

Population density:
people per sq. mile (sq. km)
Under 5 (2)
5–25 (2–10)
25–100 (10–40)
100–500 (40–200)
Over 500 (200)

0 200 400 600 km
0 100 200 300 400 mi

©DIAGRAM

9

The languages of East Africa

The people of East Africa speak a wide variety of "home" languages, because each country, with the exception of Somalia, contains many ethnic groups, each speaking its own language. In addition, people often use the language of their former colonial power, such as English or French, while many Muslims learn Arabic, the language of the Islamic holy book, the Koran. As a result, many East Africans are multilingual.

To bring some order to this linguistic richness, each country has at least one official language. Thus in Kenya, Tanzania, and Uganda, the official languages are Swahili – an important trading language in the region – and English, the language of the former colonial power, with many people also speaking one of the numerous Bantu languages, such as Ganda or Kikuyu. English is also the official language of Malawi, where people also speak a Bantu language, such as Chewa. It is also spoken in the Seychelles, where the official language is a French Creole language known as Seselwa. The Asian population of East Africa also speak one of the languages of the subcontinent, such as Gujarati or Punjabi.

In the former Belgian colonies of Burundi and Rwanda, French is the official language alongside Kirundi in Burundi and Kinyarwanda in Rwanda, both Bantu languages. French is also one of the two official languages in Djibouti, alongside Arabic. In neighboring Somalia, the two official languages are Arabic and Somali, but the ill-defined borders and nomadic lifestyle of many people in the Horn of Africa mean that Somali is spoken widely in both Djibouti and Ethiopia.

The most ethnically diverse country in the region is Ethiopia, where there are more than 70 distinct ethnic groups speaking more than 280 languages altogether. The official language of this multiethnic country is Amharic. In neighboring Eritrea, the official language is Tigrinya, although here, too, many other home languages are spoken.

ለ፡ወእጠየቅ፡ታሎ፡ወይቢ
ሎ፡ሶበ፡ታቀርብ፡ቀርበንክ።
ደበ፡ምሥዋዕ፡ወተዘእር
ክ፡በህየ፡ክመቦ፡ህየ፡እኔ
ክ፡ዘየንይስክ፡ላዳግ፡ህየ
ቀርበናቲክ፡ወተዐረት፡ም
ስለ፡እኖክ።ወዶእዚኔ፡አ
ንክ፡እሬኢ፡ብዙጋን፡ይትመ
ጠዉ፡ሥጋሁ፡ለእገዚእነ፡
ክርስቶስ።እሞ፡እንክ፡ተ
በወሐ፡ለሐዊር፡እንዘ፡ይት
ልዉ፡በዝነቲ፡ልግደ፡ዘእ
ልቦ፡ሕግ፡ይገብሩ፡ክመዝ፡
ሶበ፡በጽሐ፡ጸመ፡ፋሲካ።
ወእመፋትው፡ይንጽሩ፡ጸ
መ፡በዓላት፡ዘእንበለ፡እን
ጽሐ፡ነፍስ፡ወሥጋ።ወእ
ምደሳሬ፡ዘንቴ፡ይትመጠዉ፡
እምሥጠራተ፡ትደሳቲ።

Amharic script
This script developed in Ethiopia over 2,000 years ago and it is still used today. It is a modified version of an ancient Arabian script.

African languages

The people of Africa speak more than 1,000 different languages, most of them "home" languages native to the continent. The remaining languages, such as Arabic, English, or French, have all been introduced by settlers or invaders from Asia or Europe. The home languages are divided into four main families, within which are several subfamilies. These are then divided into groups and again into subgroups. Those languages spoken in East Africa are printed in *italic* type below.

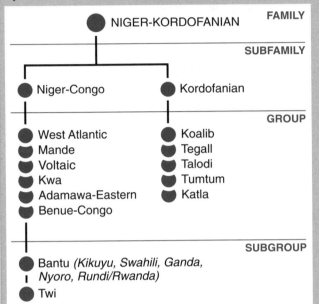

NIGER-KORDOFANIAN — **FAMILY**

SUBFAMILY
- Niger-Congo
- Kordofanian

GROUP
- West Atlantic
- Mande
- Voltaic
- Kwa
- Adamawa-Eastern
- Benue-Congo

- Koalib
- Tegall
- Talodi
- Tumtum
- Katla

SUBGROUP
- Bantu *(Kikuyu, Swahili, Ganda, Nyoro, Rundi/Rwanda)*
- Twi

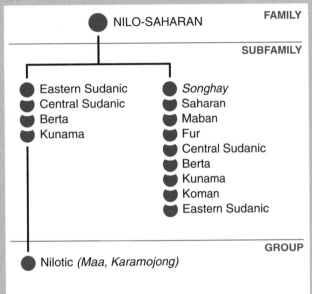

NILO-SAHARAN — **FAMILY**

SUBFAMILY
- Eastern Sudanic
- Central Sudanic
- Berta
- Kunama

- *Songhay*
- Saharan
- Maban
- Fur
- Central Sudanic
- Berta
- Kunama
- Koman
- Eastern Sudanic

GROUP
- Nilotic *(Maa, Karamojong)*

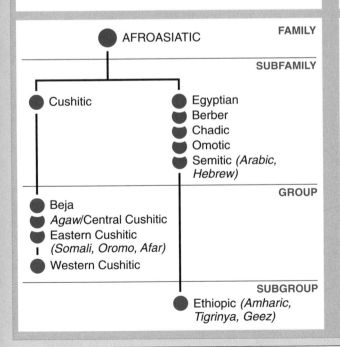

AFROASIATIC — **FAMILY**

SUBFAMILY
- Cushitic

- Egyptian
- Berber
- Chadic
- Omotic
- Semitic *(Arabic, Hebrew)*

GROUP
- Beja
- *Agaw*/Central Cushitic
- Eastern Cushitic *(Somali, Oromo, Afar)*
- Western Cushitic

SUBGROUP
- Ethiopic *(Amharic, Tigrinya, Geez)*

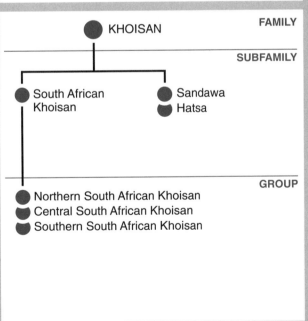

KHOISAN — **FAMILY**

SUBFAMILY
- South African Khoisan

- Sandawa
- Hatsa

GROUP
- Northern South African Khoisan
- Central South African Khoisan
- Southern South African Khoisan

© DIAGRAM

THE HISTORY

We know about East Africa's history from a large number of sources. Fossil remains of skeletons found in the Great Rift Valley tell us that our earliest hominid ancestors may have evolved in East Africa 4.4 million years ago, while more recent skeletons show us that our oldest human ancestors flourished here some 2 million years ago. Pebble tools found in the Olduvai Gorge reveal the many skills these early hominids mastered.

In historic times, ancient buildings, stone pillars, and rock-hewn churches tell us about the ancient Christian civilization of Ethiopia, while forts and other buildings along the east coast show us how important the region was to the flourishing trade routes of the Indian Ocean.

The many different peoples of the region have all left sculptures, carvings, and other artifacts behind them, while Arab and European colonialists have left their mark on the region in the form of buildings, railway lines, dams, and other works of engineering. European explorers searching for the source of the Nile and missionaries wishing to convert local people to Christianity all wrote journals and diaries, telling us much about the local civilizations they encountered, while many documents, and scholarly works of history, religion, and politics have been preserved in libraries, churches, monasteries, and mosques.

Most importantly, myths, legends, and tales passed down by word of mouth through the generations have enabled us to catch a glimpse of what life was like for many people in the region hundreds of years ago.

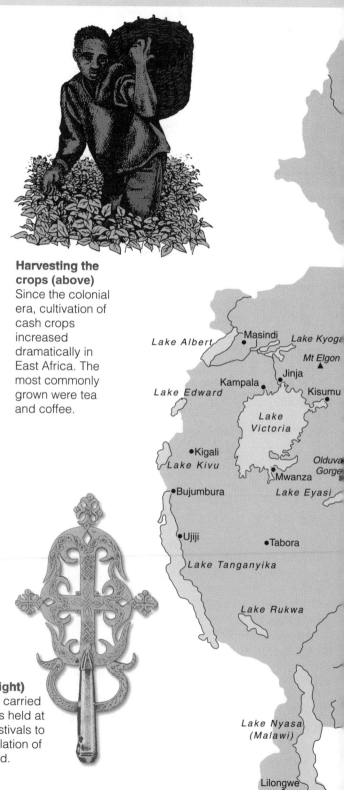

Harvesting the crops (above)
Since the colonial era, cultivation of cash crops increased dramatically in East Africa. The most commonly grown were tea and coffee.

Processional cross (right)
Decorative crosses are carried in Christian processions held at Christmas and other festivals to commemorate the revelation of Jesus as the Son of God.

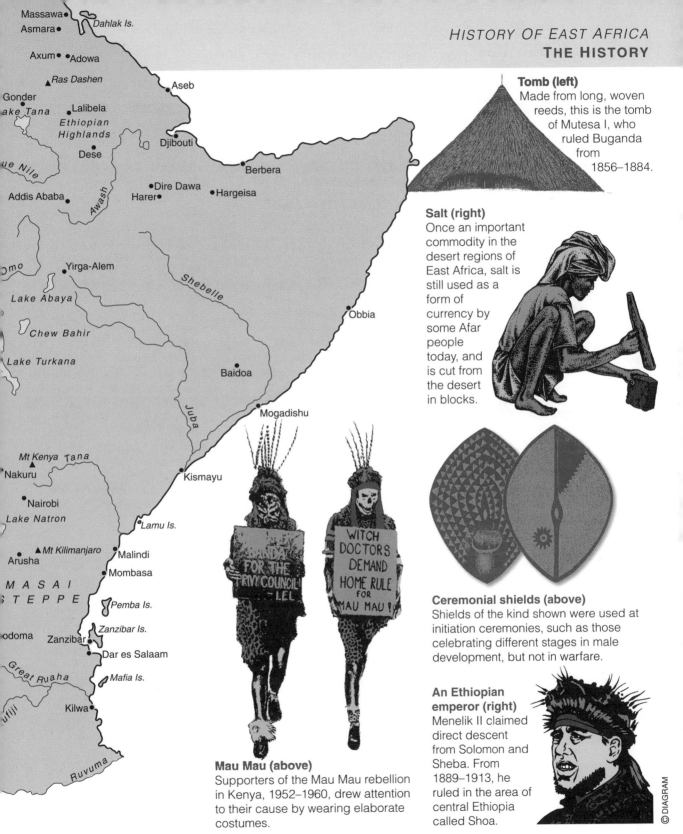

Massawa
Asmara
Dahlak Is.
Axum **Adowa**
▲ *Ras Dashen*
Gonder
ake Tana
Lalibela
Ethiopian Highlands
Dese
ue Nile
Addis Ababa
Awash
Aseb
Djibouti
Berbera
Dire Dawa
Harer **Hargeisa**
Obbia
mo
Yirga-Alem
Shebelle
Lake Abaya
Chew Bahir
Lake Turkana
Baidoa
Juba
Mogadishu
▲ *Mt Kenya* *Tana*
Nakuru
Nairobi
Lake Natron
Kismayu
Lamu Is.
▲ *Mt Kilimanjaro*
Arusha
Malindi
Mombasa
M A S A I
S T E P P E
Pemba Is.
Zanzibar Is.
odoma
Zanzibar
Dar es Salaam
Mafia Is.
Great Ruaha
ufiji
Kilwa
Ruvuma

Tomb (left)
Made from long, woven reeds, this is the tomb of Mutesa I, who ruled Buganda from 1856–1884.

Salt (right)
Once an important commodity in the desert regions of East Africa, salt is still used as a form of currency by some Afar people today, and is cut from the desert in blocks.

Mau Mau (above)
Supporters of the Mau Mau rebellion in Kenya, 1952–1960, drew attention to their cause by wearing elaborate costumes.

Ceremonial shields (above)
Shields of the kind shown were used at initiation ceremonies, such as those celebrating different stages in male development, but not in warfare.

An Ethiopian emperor (right)
Menelik II claimed direct descent from Solomon and Sheba. From 1889–1913, he ruled in the area of central Ethiopia called Shoa.

© DIAGRAM

13

Historical events

EAST AFRICAN EVENTS

1851–1900

1859–1870	Bunyoro and Toro kingdoms at war
1856	Zanzibar becomes an independent sultanate
1873	Zanzibar slave market closes
1883	Italians take Eritrean port of Aseb
1884	French Somaliland (Djibouti) and British Somaliland (Somalia) established
1885	Germans occupy Tanganyika (Tanzania)
1888	British first occupy Buganda (Uganda)
1889	Italian Somaliland (Somalia) established
1889	Italians occupy whole of Eritrea
1890	Anglo-German agreement defines European spheres of influence in East Africa; Germans occupy Burundi and Rwanda; Britain takes control of Zanzibar
1891	British declare a protectorate (colony) over Nyasaland (Malawi)
1894	British establish a protectorate over Buganda
1896	Italians defeated by Ethiopians at battle of Adowa; Ethiopia conquers Oromo kingdoms
1896	Bunyoro and Toro kingdoms made British protectorates (Uganda)

1901–1945

1916	Ruanda and Urundi occupied by Belgium
1918	British occupy German-owned Tanganyika
1930	Haile Selassie becomes emperor of Ethiopia
1935–1941	Italian forces invade and occupy Ethiopia
1941	Italians driven out of Ethiopia, Eritrea, and Somaliland by British

1946–1970

1952	Eritrea federated to Ethiopia
1952–1960	Mau Mau rebellion in Kenya against British rule
1960–1964	All of East Africa apart from Djibouti and Seychelles gain independence from European colonial rule
1961	Eritrean rebels begin armed struggle for independence
1963	Hastings Banda becomes prime minister in Malawi
1964	Tanganyika and Zanzibar unite to form Tanzania
1966	Military coup in Burundi
1967	Milton Obote takes power as president of Uganda
1967	Traditional kingdoms abolished in Uganda
1967	French Somaliland becomes French Territory of the Afars and the Issas
1967	Kenya, Uganda, and Tanzania set up East African Community
1969	Military coup in Somalia led by Maj.-Gen. Muhammad Siad Barre

WORLD EVENTS

1861–1865 US Civil War
1865 USA abolishes slavery
1869 Suez Canal opened
1871 Germany united
1875 Egypt sells its shares in the Suez Canal to Britain
1881 French rule begins in Tunisia
1882 British rule begins in Egypt
1882 Anglo-Egyptian forces conquer Sudan

1905 First Russian Revolution
1911 Chinese Revolution
1917 USA enters World War I
1939 Germany invades Poland, starting World War II
1945 United Nations established

1948 Israel founded
1949 Western nations set up North Atlantic Treaty NATO
1955 Warsaw Pact set up in eastern Europe
1956 USSR crushes Hungarian uprising
1957 European Common Market, later the European Union, set up
1960 Organization of Petroleum Exporting Countries (OPEC) formed
1961 Berlin Wall divides city
1963 Organization of African Unity (OAU) founded
1963 President Kennedy assassinated
1965–1973 US troops fight in Vietnam

Colonial occupation and independence

EAST AFRICAN EVENTS

1971–1980

1971 Colonel Amin seizes power in Uganda; Banda becomes president of Malawi

1972 Hutus in Burundi revolt against Tutsi elite; civil war breaks out and 200,000 Hutus are killed

1972 80,000 Asians expelled from Uganda

1973 Military coup in Rwanda

1974 Haile Selassie overthrown by army in Ethiopia

1976 Peaceful coup in Burundi

1977 One year after independence, army takes power in Seychelles

1977 Haile Mariam Mengistu takes power in Ethiopia and initiates land reform; conflict between Somalia and Ethiopia over Ogaden region

1977 East African Community dissolved

1977 Djibouti gains independence from France

1978 Uganda invades Tanzania

1979 Tanzanian and Ugandan forces oust Amin

1981–1990

1980s Ethiopia and Somalia hold talks to end conflict over Ogaden region

1981 Somali National Movement (SNM) begins guerrilla activities

1981–1986 Ugandan civil war; rebels led by Yoweri Museveni win power

1984–1985 Falashas airlifted from Ethiopia to Israel

1985 Military coup in Uganda

1986 Rebels oust military in Uganda

1987 Military coup in Burundi; clashes between Hutus and Tutsis

1991–2002

1991 Afar rebels in Djibouti demand multiparty politics

1991 Mengistu loses control of Ethiopia; civil war comes to an end

1991 Ugandan Asians invited to return

1991 Civil war breaks out in Somalia after Siad Barre is ousted by rebel clan groups; former British Somaliland declares independence as Somaliland Republic; famine breaks out in the country

1992 UN and USA intervene in Somalia

1992 Traditional monarchies restored in Uganda; nonparty elections held

1993 Eritrea becomes independent

1994 Afar rebels sign peace accord in Djibouti

1994 Rwanda and Burundi Hutu presidents assassinated

1994 Ethiopian war crimes trials begin

1994 Genocide in Rwanda as 750,000 Tutsi killed

1995 Hutu-Tutsi violence spreads to Burundi; massacres

WORLD EVENTS

1973 Yom Kippur War between Egypt and Israel

1974 Revolution in Portugal leads to its withdrawal from its African colonies

1975 End of Vietnam War as country is united

1979 Camp David talks end state of war between Egypt and Israel

1979 Islamic fundamentalists take power in Iran

1979 USSR invades Afghanistan

1980–1988 Iran-Iraq War

1988 Libya suspected of bombing Pan-Am aircraft that explodes over Scotland

1989 Tiananmen Square massacre in China

1990–1991 Gulf War after Iraq invades Kuwait

1990–1991 Collapse of communism in eastern Europe and USSR

1991–1995 War in Yugoslavia as country breaks up

1994 Multiparty elections in South Africa end apartheid

1998 Good Friday agreement brings peace to Northern Ireland

2001 One of the two Libyans suspected of 1988 Pan Am bombing found guilty

2001 Terrorist attack on World Trade Center in New York leads to invasion of Afghanistan

2002 African Union set up to replace ailing Organization of African Unity (OAU)

EAST AFRICAN EVENTS

	at Hutu refugee camp in Rwanda; many Hutus flee to neighboring Zaïre
1995	Richard Leakey forms Safina party in Kenya
1995	Ugandan troops clash with Sudanese army
1995	Rwandan war crimes tribunal set up; violence escalates in Burundi leading to military coup
1996	Violence escalating in Burundi
1998–2000	Border dispute between Eritrea and Ethiopia
1998	US embassies in Nairobi, Kenya, and Dar es Salaam, Tanzania bombed by Islamic extremists
2001	Peace agreement signed in Burundi; provisional government including members of all groups set up
2002	International arbitration ends Eritrean-Ethiopian border dispute; conflict continues in Burundi; terrorist bomb kills 11 in Kenya

Dar es Salaam bomb
Tanzania's first major terrorist attack took place in August 1998.

COLONIAL OCCUPATION AND INDEPENDENCE

Country	Independence	Occupied*	Colonial powers
Burundi (as part of Ruanda-Urundi)	July 1, 1962	1890	Germany 1890–1919; Belgium 1919–1962
Djibouti (as French Somaliland then French Territory of the Afars and the Issas)	June 27, 1977	1884	France
Eritrea	May 24, 1993	1889	Italy 1889–1941; Britain 1941–1952; ruled by Ethiopia 1952–1993
Kenya	Dec 12, 1963	1895	Britain
Malawi (as Nyasaland)	July 6, 1964	1891	Britain
Rwanda (as part of Ruanda-Urundi)	July 1, 1962	1890	Germany 1890–1919; Belgium 1919–1962
Seychelles	June 29, 1976	1742	France 1742–1814; Britain 1814–1976
Somalia (As British Somaliland)	June 26, 1960	1884	Britain
Somalia (As Italian Somaliland)	July 1, 1960	1889	Italy 1889–1941; 1950–1960; Britain 1941–1950
Tanzania (as Tanganyika)	Dec 9, 1961	1885	Germany 1885–1920; Britain 1920–1961
Tanzania (Zanzibar)	Dec 10, 1963	1890	Britain
Uganda (as Uganda Protectorate)	Oct 9, 1962	1888	Britain

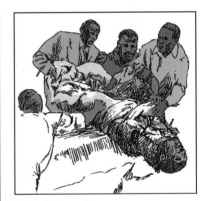

Nairobi bomb
An explosion in Nairobi in 1998 killed over 230 people and wounded thousands more.

* The years given for the beginning of colonial occupation of the modern-day nations are those by which a significant area of coastal and hinterland territory had been effectively occupied by a colonial power.

© DIAGRAM

THE CRADLE OF HUMANITY

Olduvai Gorge now
This is a deep cleft in the ground in the Great Rift Valley in Africa with cliffs reaching as high as 330 ft (130 m). Campsites, toolkits, and other artifacts found in the vicinity suggest that the earliest human settlements may have been located in the Gorge nearly two million years ago.

The Great Rift Valley is a major geological feature in the Earth's surface that runs some 3,000 miles (4,830 km) south from Syria in western Asia to Mozambique in southern Africa. The importance of this valley in human evolution is that, along its length, evidence of the first hominids and humans has been found, suggesting that the valley acted both as a nursery in which our ancestors evolved and developed, and a huge corridor along which they traveled through Africa and into Asia.

Forming the rift

The Great Rift Valley was formed by movements in the Earth's hard outer layers (the crust and the top of the mantle). These movements stretched the land of Africa creating long faults in the land. As the stretching continued, a huge chunk of land sank between the faults, creating a broad, steep-sided valley. The valley, in its present form, has existed for the last 2 million years.

The Great Rift Valley starts in northern Syria and then runs down through the Jordan Valley and the Dead Sea to the Gulf of Aqaba and on into the Red Sea. It cuts through Ethiopia and follows a southerly course through Kenya and Tanzania into Malawi to the lower Zambezi valley in

Mozambique. Many East African lakes, such as Nyasa and Turkana, lie on the Valley floor. A western branch of the Valley runs from the northern tip of Lake Nyasa (also called Lake Malawi), through lakes Tanganyika, Kivu, Edward, and Albert. Lake Victoria, Africa's largest lake, occupies a shallow depression in the high plateau between the two arms of the Rift Valley.

The Great Rift Valley ranges in elevation from about 1,300 ft (395 m) below sea level in the Dead Sea to about 6,000 ft (1,830 m) above sea level in southern Kenya. Much of it is has been concealed by centuries of erosion, but in several places, notably Kenya, sheer cliffs either side of the rift rise for several thousand feet.

Olduvai Gorge

Olduvai Gorge, in northern Tanzania, is a deep cleft in the ground of the Rift Valley. Its cliffs are 300 ft (130 m) high and show layers of rock dating between 600,000 and 1.8 million years old. In this gorge, remains of three species of hominids, as well as stone tools and an early settlement, all suggest that the gorge was home to some of our earliest ancestors, who learned skills here that were necessary for them to survive elsewhere in the world.

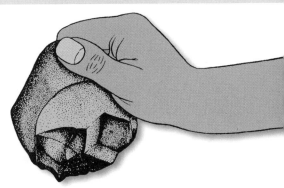

Artifact
This pebble tool was probably used as a chopper for cutting meat or cracking open bones. Found at Olduvai Gorge in northern Tanzania, it was probably made by *Homo habilis* 2.5 million years ago.

Olduvai Gorge then (below)
Ths is an impression of how the Gorge probably looked 2 million years ago. There were small lakes and swamps, extinct volcanoes, and a variety of animals, such as baboons, antelopes, and zebras. The panoramic scene shown here is overlooked by some of our earliest human ancestors.

© DIAGRAM

The earliest hominids

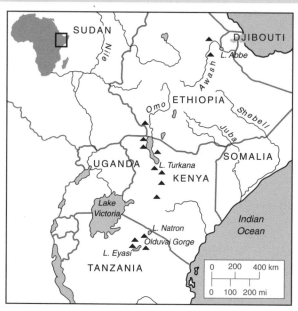

Over 100 years ago, Charles Darwin, the British naturalist and author of *On The Origin of Species*, suggested that human beings first evolved in Africa. We now know this to be true, because a number of scientific discoveries, made in the 1950s, narrowed the habitat of the earliest human beings, and their immediate ancestors, down to East Africa and, in particular, along the Great Rift Valley in Ethiopia, Kenya, and Tanzania.

The forerunners of present-day human beings are known collectively as hominids, from the Latin word *homo*, meaning man. Scientists group humans, hominids, apes, monkeys, and several other animals, such as lemurs, together as primates. They believe that all primates had a common ancestor which lived in East Africa over 5 million years ago.

Fossilized bones of several of the earliest known hominids were discovered in eastern Ethiopia by American anthropologists in 1992–1994. The creature has been named *Australopithecus ramidus* – *Australopithecus* means "southern ape," *ramidus* means "root" in the language of the Afar people of the area. This species lived about 4.4 million years ago, half a million years before the earliest hominid discovered up until that point.

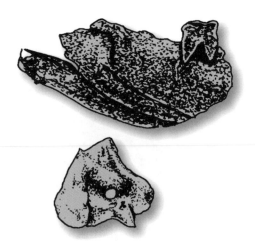

Fossil finds
These two pieces of bone possibly originated from early australopiths. The jawbone (top) is probably 5.5 million years old and was discovered in Lothagam, Kenya. The elbow joint (bottom) is probably 4 million years old and comes from Kanapoi in Kenya.

Lucy's skeleton
Discovered in Ethiopia in 1974, this 3 million-year-old skeleton became the oldest known for any hominid.

Here's Lucy!

Several species of australopithecines have been found, some in East Africa and some in southern Africa. Before *A. ramidus*, the oldest known hominid was *Australopithecus afarensis* ("southern ape of the Afar"). In 1974 a partial three-million-year-old *A. afarensis* skeleton was found in the Afar region of northern Ethiopia and was nicknamed Lucy. Both *A. ramidus* and *A. afarensis* were lightly built and only about 4 ft (1.3 m) tall. So was the next oldest species of hominid, *Australopithecus africanus*, which probably lived from three million to two and a half million years ago. A later species, *Paranthropus boisei* – named after the British industrialist, Charles Boise, who funded East African fossil hunts – was discovered in East Africa in 1959.

Body build (below)

A male and female of each of the following species of hominids, the forerunners of present-day humans, are shown beside a modern man for comparison. From left to right, the species are *Australopithecus afarensis* (**A**), *Australopithecus africanus* (**B**), *Paranthropus boisei* (**C**), and *Paranthropus robustus* (**D**). *Australopithecus afarensis* probably lived 3 million years ago, *Australopithecus africanus* 3 to 2.4 million years ago, *Paranthropus boisei* 2.3 to 1.4 million years ago, and *Paranthropus robustus* probably evolved 1.8 million years ago.

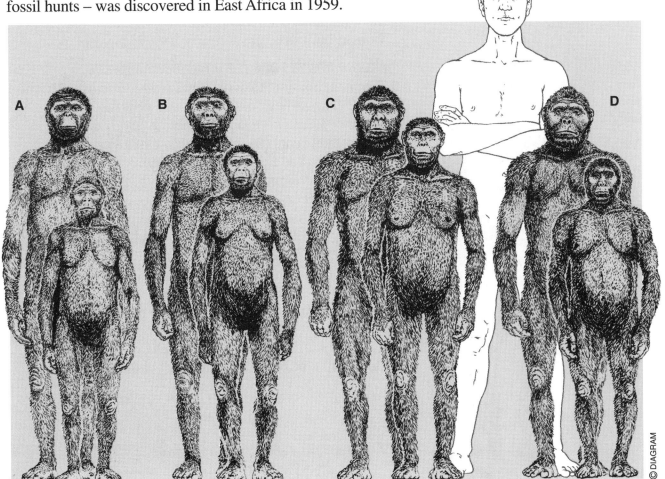

A   B   C   D

© DIAGRAM

The first humans

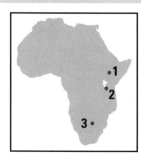

Where *habilis* lived
This map shows the sites where *H. habilis* probably lived.
1 Koobi Fora
2 Olduvai Gorge
3 Swartkrans
There are also claims for other sites in East Africa.

After the australopithecines, all our supposed ancestors are grouped in the scientific genus *Homo*. The first-known species of *Homo* was *habilis*, or "handyman." *Homo habilis* remains were discovered in Tanzania in 1961, and are probably about 2 million years old. It is thought that the earliest known toolkit, containing pebbles chipped into tool-like shapes, was made by *Homo habilis*. These and other artifacts from what is known as the Oldowan Culture have been found in the Olduvai Gorge in Tanzania in East Africa

Homo habilis is also believed to have hunted food and built shelters to live in. Evidence of early campsites suggests that the earliest human settlements might have been at Olduvai Gorge. The remains of very early fences and even a stone circle that was probably the foundation for a hut have been found, making it the oldest known human-built structure at nearly 2 millions years old.

Homo erectus and *Homo sapiens sapiens*

The next hominid to evolve was *Homo erectus*, "upright man." The earliest fossil was found near the western shore of Lake Turkana in northern Kenya, and is about 1.8 million years old. *Homo erectus* had a cranium with a heavily-browed ridge and perhaps grew up to 6 ft (1.8 m), as tall as a present-day human.

Homo erectus spread from East Africa up the Rift Valley into Asia and then Europe, and persisted until as recently as 50,000 years ago. Modern humans belong to the species *Home sapiens sapiens* and are almost certainly descended from *Homo erectus*. The earliest known fossils of fully modern *Homo sapiens sapiens* have been found at Omo in southern Ethiopia, as well as sites in South Africa and Israel, and date from about 110,000 BCE. By then, *Homo sapiens sapiens* was the dominant type of human, replacing earlier species.

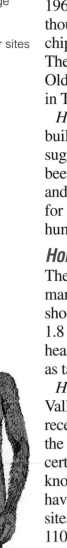

Body build (left)
A male and female *Homo habilis* are shown beside a modern man. *H. habilis* probably lived about 2.4 to 1.6 million years ago.

The fossil hunters

Much of the research into the existence of early humans in East Africa was carried out by the Anglo-Kenyan anthropologists, the Leakey family: Louis, Mary, and their sons Richard and Jonathan.

Louis Leakey was a Kenyan, the son of British missionaries. With Mary, and later Richard, he found important fossil remains in East Africa, especially in Olduvai Gorge, including the remains of *Homo habilis*.

Mary was born in England but moved to Kenya after marrying Louis in 1936. In 1948 she discovered the fossil remains of a primitive ape thought to have lived 25–40 million years ago. Together with her husband she made many other important discoveries.

Richard Leakey has achieved international fame both as an anthropologist and, in 1989, as Kenya National Parks director of wildlife management, where he made great attempts to protect the wildlife from poaching. In 1995 he set up a political party to challenge the personal and autocratic rule of President Moi.

Alongside the Leakeys, a team of Kenyan coworkers made equally important discoveries. In 1984 Kamoya Kimeu discovered a 1.5-million-year-old *Homo erectus* skeleton near Lake Turkana.

Body build (below)
A male and female *Home erectus* are shown beside a modern man for comparison. *Erectus* probably lived from about 1.8 million years ago until as recently as 50,000 BCE.

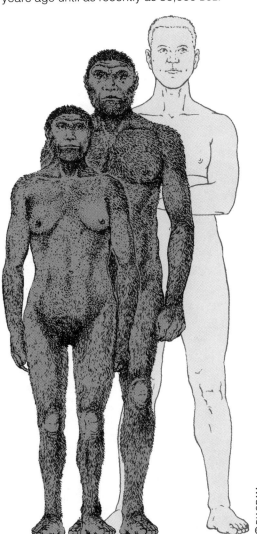

Louis Leakey (above)
He found fossil remains, including *Homo habilis*, in Olduvai Gorge.

Mary Leakey (above)
She discovered fossil remains of an ape believed over 25–40 million years old.

Kamoya Kimeu (left)
He was well known for this ability to uncover the smallest fragments of hominid fossils ever found.

© DIAGRAM

23

The first farmers

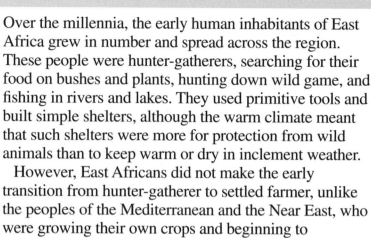

A glimpse of the past
The preserved remains of ancient tools and equipment suggest ways in which East African land was farmed c.3,500 BCE. The wooden stick (left) was used for digging up roots and tubers, while the knife (far right) would have been used for reaping crops. Small blades were inserted into the slotted wooden stick, and held in position, using small lengths of rope, to provide a sharp cutting edge.

Over the millennia, the early human inhabitants of East Africa grew in number and spread across the region. These people were hunter-gatherers, searching for their food on bushes and plants, hunting down wild game, and fishing in rivers and lakes. They used primitive tools and built simple shelters, although the warm climate meant that such shelters were more for protection from wild animals than to keep warm or dry in inclement weather.

However, East Africans did not make the early transition from hunter-gatherer to settled farmer, unlike the peoples of the Mediterranean and the Near East, who were growing their own crops and beginning to domesticate their own livestock from about 8000 BCE. While cattle were domesticated in the Nile Valley in Egypt by 3000 BCE, that skill did not spread south into Ethiopia or Somalia until about 1000 BCE, and it was not until 300 CE that cattle were domesticated around Lake Victoria and 750 CE along the east coast.

Growing crops

East African people were far later than their northern relations in growing crops. Archaeological evidence

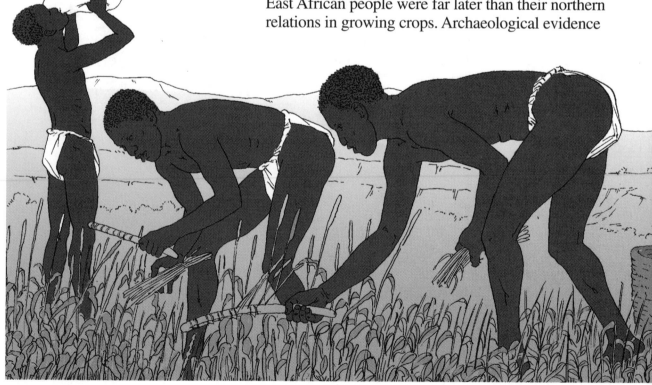

suggests that knowledge of farming spread south along the fertile Rift Valley corridor into southern Ethiopia and around Lake Victoria about 3500 BCE. The early farmers in this region grew finger millet, teff (a small grain), ensete (the plant cultivated not for its fruit but its stem and root), and other crops native to the region. Most of these crops were tubers and tree crops rather than cereals, such as wheat and barley, since cereals mostly require winter rainfall to irrigate the ground, not summer rainfall that would wash them away. Cereal growing was thus restricted to the more temperate Ethiopian highlands, where barley was grown at Lalibela in c.500 BCE and other cereals were also grown and harvested.

Settled farming in parts of the region, however, was difficult, because of the dense rainforest vegetation around the Great Lakes and the arid deserts in the Horn of Africa. The lack of suitable iron tools was an additional problem, as it meant that farmers had no proper tools to clear the ground for planting crops or grazing animals. As a result, farming was not nearly as developed as in North Africa, and thus the population remained smaller because less food was produced. Most people remained hunter-gatherers, living off the abundant wildlife and lush vegetation available in most of the region.

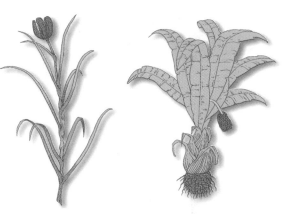

Native African crops
Finger millet (above left) is one of six species of cultivated African millets. Ensete (above right) is cultivated for its stem and tap root rather than its fruit.

Gathering food
Hunting and gathering as a means of subsistence remained important in Africa, particularly in the south and west of the continent, for a long time after pastoralism and farming had taken over in Europe, western Asia or the Far East. Communities freely harvested the available plant resources using their basic tools and equipment.

© DIAGRAM

From about 500 BCE, three groups of people began to migrate into East Africa: the Bantu-speaking peoples, Cushites, and Nilotes. These groupings are based on cultural and linguistic similarities and comprise the ancestors of most present-day East Africans.

The movement of these people is still subject to great controversy, as the evidence is scarce and accurate dating is hard to achieve. In the absence of any written record or artifact, most of what we know of this period has come to us through detailed linguistic analysis.

Bantus

The first major group of people to settle in East Africa were Bantu speakers, who originated in eastern Nigeria and had settled in the Congo river basin in about 500 BCE.

Five hundred years later, Bantu-speaking people had spread west to the Atlantic Ocean, and east across the continent to reach the Indian Ocean in southern Tanzania and northern Mozambique. From there, they spread northwards along the coast and up through the Great Lakes, and south into the Zambezi river valley of southern Africa, eventually occupying and dominating the whole of Africa south of the equator apart from the far southwest by 1000 CE.

Not every linguist or historian accepts this proposed migration route, suggesting instead that Bantu speakers first arrived in the area north of the Great Lakes and then

Ceremonial attire
This man is a member of the Kikuyu, a group of people descended from the Bantu speakers originating in Nigeria. He is shown here in traditional costume, as opposed to his normal Western-style clothing.

Maasai herdsmen and their cattle (left)
Most Maasai are semi-nomadic pastoralists – livestock traders who move seasonally with their herds to make the best use of available water and pasture – who herd mostly cattle and also keep a few sheep or goats. Each family has its own cattle, but they are managed as part of a larger village herd. During the dry season, the Maasai men drive the cattle to distant watering holes, making temporary camps until the rains come.

spread south and west into southern Africa. Whichever route they took, they came to dominate East Africa, killing or assimilating the original inhabitants, who were similar to the Khoisan peoples of the south.

The modern-day, Bantu-speaking people of the Ganda, Kikuyu, Nyoro, Hutu, and Tutsi groups are all descended from these people.

Cushites and Nilotes

The other two groups of migrating people were the Cushites and Nilotes.

The Cushites originated from the Ethiopian highlands and were the first food producers in East Africa. They spread out to occupy most of northeastern Africa and some also migrated further south, reaching the Kenyan Highlands by c.1200 BCE. The modern-day Oromo of Ethiopia and northern Kenya are descended from these migrants.

The Nilotes originated from the southern borders of the Ethiopian highlands – the Nile River region of southern Sudan. The Nilotes are divided into two branches based on where they migrated to: the Highland-Plain Nilotes, such as the Maasai and Karamojong, who are also part-Cushitic, who settled in the region after 1000 CE, and the River-Lake Nilotes, such as the Luo, who settled in the region after 1400 CE.

The Nilotes were pastoralists, deriving their livelihood from herding cattle and goats.

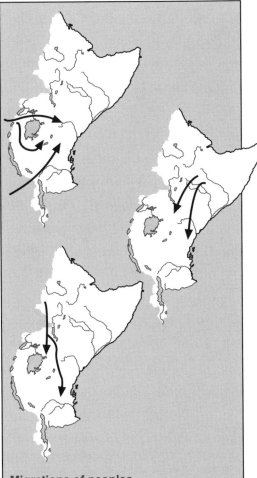

Migrations of peoples
These maps show the movement into East Africa of the following groups: Bantu, 0–1000 BCE (top); Cushites, 1200–1500 BCE (center); and Nilotes, 1000–1800 BCE (bottom).

©DIAGRAM

The ironworkers

The importance of iron technology – smelting iron ore and fashioning the smelted iron into finished objects – is that it allows farmers to make hard-wearing tools to help them in their work. Primitive iron picks, spades, and hoes are far tougher than their wooden equivalents.

Iron tools enabled farmers to dig a ditch to drain or irrigate the ground, and to till the soil ready to plant the crops. In the dense rainforest conditions of parts of East Africa, iron axes were useful for chopping down trees, clearing the undergrowth, and preparing fields for crops to be grown or livestock to graze.

Ironworking arrived in East Africa from two sources. In the north, the knowledge of iron spread up the Nile Valley from Egypt into Sudan, reaching the kingdom of Axum in Ethiopia by 400 BCE. In the rest of the region, the migrating Bantu-speakers brought iron technology with them from west and central Africa. The first area to benefit from this skill was to the west and north of Lake Victoria, by about 300 BCE.

Over the next millennium, iron was worked on the coastline and in the south of the Great Lakes region. The earliest evidence of ironworking has been found at Katuruka on the southwest shore of Lake Victoria dating back to the late 5th century BCE.

charcoal

iron ore

draft   draft

Sites at Urewe on the northeast shore of the lake, at Kalambo at the south of Lake Tanganyika, and also at Kwale on the coast north of Zanzibar are more recent, most of them dating from around 300 BCE.

Iron smelting (right)
Iron ore was placed within dome or funnel-shaped structures (right) with charcoal fuel in alternate layers of charcoal and iron ore. Many furnaces were fired using bellows, but others were designed so that the high temperature required could be reached by means of a draft directed into the center of the furnace using clay pipes. The resulting metal was usually of a very high standard.

Ironworking

Unlike Europe, East Africa went straight from the Stone Age to the Iron Age without any intervening Copper or Bronze Ages. The iron was smelted in anything from simple pits or trenches to large funnel-shaped, or domed, structures built of clay bricks. Iron ore and charcoal were placed in alternate layers inside the furnace and then heated to a temperature of over 2000°F. The furnace was fired by draughts of air sucked in through clay pipes, although bellows were often used to increase the air-flow.

The resulting iron – technically a high-carbon steel – was of a high quality. Although smelting was a labor-intensive industry consuming vast amounts of wood to make the charcoal, as well as requiring miners to quarry and extract the iron ore, there is evidence to show that iron production in the region was on a massive scale.

The introduction of iron tools brought huge benefits to East Africa. Farmers could now grow crops more productively, increase their yields, and clear more ground on which to keep their livestock. As a result, increased food production enabled the population to rise, paving the way for settled farming communities in East Africa by 800 CE.

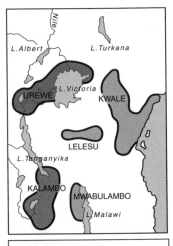

Early Iron-Age site grouping (Urewe) 300 BCE

Western stream Iron-Age site groupings 1–600 CE

Eastern stream Iron-Age site groupings 1–600 CE

Metal technology (above)
This map shows the probable spread of Bantu metal technology during the period from c.300 BCE – 600 CE.

Legacy (below)
These implements, made by Sotho-Tswana people in the late 18th century, bear witness to the inherited skills handed down from the Iron Age workers.

Operating the bellows (left)
Two assistants to the metalsmith operate the bellows for a traditional furnace designed for smelting iron. Such methods are still used by certain peoples in places like Zimbabwe today.

© DIAGRAM

ETHIOPIA AND ITS NEIGHBORS

Egyptian exploration
By 3500 years ago Egyptian wooden ships sailed south down the Red Sea to the Land of Punt (modern-day Somalia).

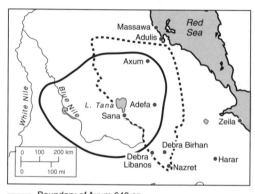

Boundary of Axum 640 CE

••••• Boundary of Axum c. 850 CE

Axumite kingdom (above)
This map shows the extent of the kingdom in 640 CE, and again in 850 CE.

Sitting woman
This limestone statue, produced in the fifth century CE, probably had some religious significance for the Axumite people.

Ethiopia is unique in Africa in that not only can it trace its history back into antiquity, as can Egypt, but that it has also retained its ancient culture and character up to the present day. Ethiopia was known to the pharaohs and merchants of Egypt more than 4,000 years ago, and maintained regular trading links with its northern and more powerful neighbor.

After the 6th century BCE, the country was much influenced by the Sabaean culture of southern Arabia, across the Red Sea; Sabaean writing survives today in the liturgical language *Ge'ez* used by the Ethiopian church. Later influences came from Ptolemaic Egypt. By around 200 BCE, the country was populated by two main groups of people, the Cushites, whose descendents include the Amhara and the Oromo, and Semitic peoples from southern Arabia.

According to tradition, the Queen of Sheba (now part of Yemen) visited King Solomon in Jerusalem and together they had a son, Menelik. Solomon allowed Menelik to make a copy of the Ark of the Covenant, one of the most sacred of Jewish objects. Menelik secretly exchanged the copy for the real Ark and took it to Axum, where he founded a kingdom, reigning between 975 and 950 BCE.

Historically, however, records date the foundation of Axum to the first century CE. The kingdom was founded

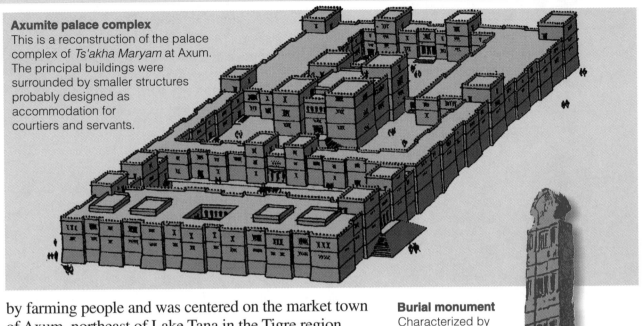

Axumite palace complex
This is a reconstruction of the palace complex of *Ts'akha Maryam* at Axum. The principal buildings were surrounded by smaller structures probably designed as accommodation for courtiers and servants.

by farming people and was centered on the market town of Axum, northeast of Lake Tana in the Tigre region.

Axum flourished as a commercial maritime nation, trading via the port of Adulis on the Red Sea, and grew so wealthy that, in the fourth century, its rulers put their own coins into circulation. The country then prospered for three centuries, dominating much of present-day Ethiopia and southern Sudan and controlling the lucrative Red Sea trade, as well as wielding great influence over southwestern Arabia.

During the fourth century, the people of Axum became Christians. The following century, the Amhara from the south of the kingdom gradually gained political dominance. The Amhara also eventually became Christian but, in 632, the power of Axum was threatened when Muslim Arabs gained control of Arabia and the Red Sea and began to restrict its trade.

The Arab conquest of Egypt by 642, and the subsequent spread of Islam up the Nile into Sudan and along the shores of the Red Sea and across the Gulf of Aden into Somalia, surrounded the Christian kingdom with hostile neighbors. The conquest ultimately strangled its foreign trade and sent the nation into a long and isolated decline.

Burial monument
Characterized by carved architectural features typical of Axumite timber and drystone buildings of the time, this monument was probably erected in the fifth century CE.

© DIAGRAM

Zagwe and Solomonid Ethiopia

Ethiopian power: from Axum to Adal	
975–950 BCE	Legendary reign of Emperor Menelik I
500s BCE–100s CE	Sabaean culture of Arabia influences Ethiopia
200 BCE	Cushites and Semitic traders live in Ethiopia
1st century CE	Foundation of Axum
300s	Axum issues gold coinage
300s–630s	Axum at height of its power and wealth
325–355	Ezana, king of Axum, converts to Christianity
400s	Amhara people become dominant in Axum and embrace Christianity
632–642	Muslim conquest of Arabia and Egypt cuts Axum off from rest of Christian world
1137	Zagwe dynasty seizes power
1270	Solomonid restoration in Ethiopia
1285	Ifat state challenges Ethiopia
1415	Ethiopia annexes Ifat
1526–1543	Adal invades Ethiopia
1543	Adal defeated and annexed

As Axum was increasingly threatened by the rising power of Islam after the seventh century, its power lessened. Axum remained a trading nation – its fleet even attacked the Arabian port of Jiddah near Mecca in 702, and its traders remained active until the 12th century – and it maintained a few possessions on the Arabian coast, such as Zabid in present-day Yemen.

But Axum was no longer the powerful state it used to be, and it retreated south into the highlands, moving its capital from Axum to Nazaret. New states around its borders threatened its survival, while its subject peoples grew restless. In 976 the Falasha, led by Queen Esato (Judith), laid waste the western part of the country.

This event seems to have been a catalyst for change, because during the 11th century the Zagwe princes from the Lasta region of central Ethiopia gradually increased their influence and power in Axum.

In 1137 the Zagwe seized power. Historians of Ethiopia have described them as not being descended from Solomon and the Queen of Sheba, but they were effective rulers. They transferred the capital to Roha (or Adefa) and did much to strengthen the Ethiopian Empire, as it was now called, waging war against rebels in the south and establishing good diplomatic relations with the powerful Muslim state of Egypt to its north.

Above all, they welcomed Coptic Christians fleeing persecution in Egypt and, under Emperor Lalibela, built a series of rock-hewn churches in the capital city, which was then named in his honor.

1

2

3

The Solomonid restoration

In 1270 the Zagwe dynasty was overthrown by Yekuno Amlak (reigned 1270–1285). Yekuno was an Amhara who claimed descent from Solomon and the Queen of Sheba through the Axumite kings, a claim supported by the influential Ethiopian church.

The restored Solomonid emperors established their capital in the southern Shoa region, expanding the empire eastward and containing Somali Muslim expansion in the southeast of the region. In response to this threat, a group of Somali sheikdoms in eastern Shoa unified under the state of Ifat in 1285. Ifat resisted Ethiopian expansion until 1328, when it became a tributary of the empire. It was finally annexed in 1415.

Under the Solomonids, Ethiopia kept up diplomatic relations with several European states, notably Aragon (which is now part of Spain), and sent delegates to various church conferences.

In 1520 the Portuguese sent an ambassador to the empire. When Ifat's successor state, Adal, began a *jihad* (Muslim holy war) against Ethiopia in 1526, and overran much of the country by 1528, the emperor Lebna Dengal (ruled 1508–1540) turned to Portugal for help. In 1541 a small Portuguese force landed in the port of Massawa, situated on the Red Sea and, on February 21, 1543, joined with an Ethiopian army to defeat the invaders and kill their leader, Ahmed Gran, at the Battle of Waina Dega. Adal was then annexed to the empire.

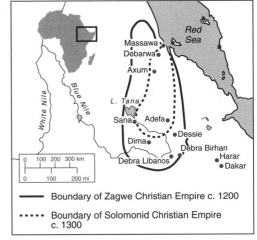

Two Christian empires
This map shows the extent of the Zagwe Christian Empire c.1200, and the Solomonid Christian empire c.1300. The Zagwe were a dynasty of Christian kings who ruled in northern and central Ethiopia during the twelfth and thirteenth centuries. In 1270 the dynasty was overthrown by Yekuno Amlak, an Amhara who claimed direct descent from Solomon and Sheba, so restoring the Solomonid empire.

Ethiopian kings and emperors
From the middle of the 13th to the end of the 16th centuries, a dynasty of kings ruled the central Ethiopian region of Shoa. The base of the empire was moved to Gondar in 1632, and the Shoan kings lost control as Muslim Oromo people migrated into their land. In 1856 the Shoa region was reincorporated into the Ethiopian Empire which was reestablished by Tewodros II.

1 Soloman and Sheba   **4** Ras Makonnen
2 Yohannes IV   **5** Haile Selassie
3 Menelik II

© DIAGRAM

Christianity in Ethiopia

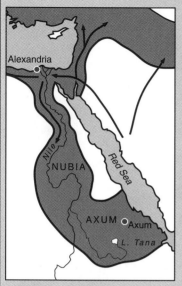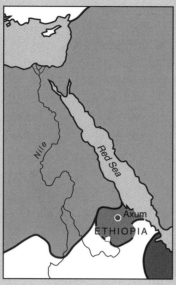

■ Christian areas
→ Arab ivasions from c. 640
■ Muslim areas

A Christian heritage (above)
Missionaries spread Christianity southward from Egypt, reaching Axum in Ethiopia about 300 CE. However, the Arab invasion in 639–642 separated the church of Axum from Alexandria in Egypt. Islam arrived in East Africa in the 800s, further isolating the Axumite Christians.

A Christian at prayer (right)
Carrying a wooden cross and staff, this pilgrim reads from the *Psalms of David*, an Ethiopian prayer book.

Christianity in Ethiopia	
c.40 CE	St Mark the Evangelist converts Alexandria to Christianity
320–355	King Ezana of Axum converts to Christianity
340s	Frumentius becomes the first Bishop of Ethiopia
451	Coptic churches split from Rome at the Council of Chalcedon
575	Nubia becomes Christian, creating a Coptic civilization the length of the Nile Valley into Axum
642	Axum cut off from the rest of Christian world by the Arab invasion of Egypt
800s	Islam arrives in East Africa
c.1185–1225	Reign of Lalibela

About half the present-day population of Ethiopia and Eritrea are Christians, heirs of an ancient religious tradition in their countries that goes back more than 1,700 years. According to tradition, St Mark the Evangelist was preaching Christianity in Alexandria, Egypt, not many years after the crucifixion of Jesus c.30 CE. The Christian church in Egypt regards him as its founder. From there, missionaries and traders spread Christianity southward from Alexandria up the Nile Valley, reaching Axum in Ethiopia by about 300 CE.

The two people who are believed to have brought Christianity into the country were the Syrian monks, called Aedesius and

Frumentius. The latter is known to Ethiopians as Abba Salama and became the first Bishop of Ethiopia during the 340s after his consecration by St Athanasius in Alexandria.

This consecration made the Ethiopian church subordinate to the Egyptian Coptic church which, after the Council of Chalcedon in 451, split from the main Christian church in Rome to become an independent church in its own right. The Coptic church believes in the unity of both the human and the divine in the nature of Christ, a unity known as the Monophysite doctrine; this doctrine is rejected by other Christian churches.

The most important convert the two Syrian monks made was the king of Axum, Ezana, who ruled from 320 to 355 CE. Under his influence, Axum became entirely Christian.

In 324 Axum defeated Meroe, its northern neighbor in Nubia (Sudan), which then broke up into three smaller kingdoms and whose inhabitants gradually became Christian. By 575 the whole of Nubia was Christian, creating a Coptic world that stretched from Alexandria in the north, to Axum and beyond in the south.

The unity of this world was shattered by the Arab invasion of Egypt in 639–642, and the rapid spread of Islam throughout North Africa.

The Coptic church of Axum was now separated from Alexandria and pursued its own course, isolated in its mountainous terrain from events in the outside world.

The arrival of Islam in East Africa during the 800s further increased its isolation.

The patron saint of Ethiopia (above)
This 19th-century illustration is taken from the 17th-century church of Debre Berhan Selassie in the Gonder region of Ethiopia. Drawn on canvas, and fixed directly onto the wall, it depicts St. George (or Ghiorgis) slaying the dragon.

A church painting (below)
This illustration shows a group of Christian clergy in ceremonial vestments, and was discovered in a church in Gonder, Ethiopia.

The rock churches of Lalibela

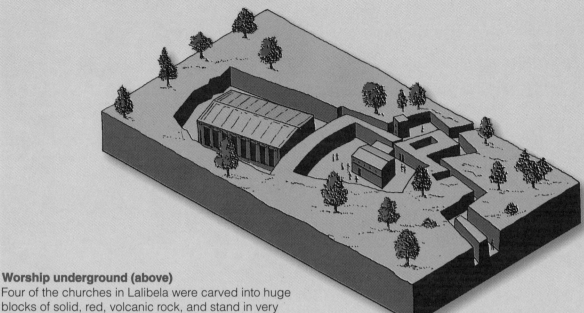

Worship underground (above)
Four of the churches in Lalibela were carved into huge blocks of solid, red, volcanic rock, and stand in very deep trenches cut into the rock.

Beta Ghiorghis (below)
This church was dedicated to St. George, the patron saint of Ethiopia, and was one of the 11 churches in Lalibela. Legend claims that the saint himself supervised its construction, and that his horse's footprints are still visible in the ditch around the church.

The heart of East African Christianity is Lalibela, which lies in rough country less than 100 miles east of Laka Tana. Under its old name of Roha (or Adefa), it was the capital city of the Zagwe dynasty. Tradition has it that, in the late 1100s, a prince was born there and christened Lalibela, and the place is now named after him.

When Lalibela became king in c.1185, he set about constructing 11 churches in the town. The churches are all cut into the solid, red, volcanic rock in three groups. Four of them are huge blocks of stone cut and carved into buildings, free-standing amid deep trenches. The other seven are more closely attached to the cliffs into which they are cut. All follow broadly a similar rectangular design, with a rectangular nave and three entrance doors at the west end facing the altar at the east. A network of artificial caves and tunnels connects the churches, which are served by about 1,000 priests and a community of nuns.

Despite the legend of Lalibela, some experts believe that at least some of the churches were begun *well before his time. One church is definitely known to be older: the church of Mekina Medahane Alem, which was built in the conventional way inside a vast cave some 300 years before Lalibela.*

Quite why the churches were built is not known, but it has been suggested that the fall of Jerusalem to the Muslims in 1187, after almost a century of Christian rule, might have prompted Lalibela to build his own Jerusalem in the hills of Ethiopia. Today, the town of Lalibela is hardly more than a village, but it is place of pilgrimage during the festivals of Genna (Christmas) and Timkat (Easter).

The art of the cross

The church of Beta Ghiorghis (the House of St George, the patron saint of Ethiopia) at Lalibela is modeled on the shape of a cross, the main symbol of Ethiopian Christian art, of which there are many elaborate designs. Craftworkers in the Axumite kingdom made early crosses of gold or iron.

When the center of government and the church moved to Lalibela, copper became the preferred metal. Later crosses, not made in Lalibela, are of wood or brass.

The designs of crosses may have been copied from those of the Coptic church of Egypt, with which the Ethiopian church has many links, and are of several designs. Tall crosses are carried in processions; pilgrims carry crosses on staves on their shoulders; men and children wear crosses around their necks, women wear crosses as pendants; and priests use handheld crosses for blessing the faithful.

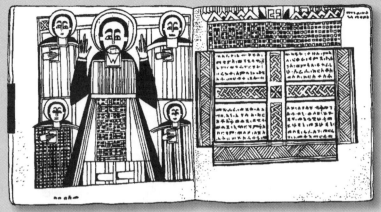

An illuminated manuscript (above)
Christ and the four evangelists are depicted on the left-hand page of this manuscript of the *Four Gospels* dating from the 1600s. The text shown on the right-hand page is written in *Ge'ez*, an ancient Ethiopian language

An Ethiopian cross (right)
This is an example of a 12th-century, intricately-worked, processional cross which would have been mounted on the end of a tall, wooden staff.

© DIAGRAM

The decline of Ethiopia

Oromo expansion
The map on the right shows the area occupied by the Oromo c.1530. The far right map reflects the situation in 1563.

■ Oromo-occupied areas

After the defeat of Adal in 1543, the Solomonid empire faced three threats. The first came from the Ottoman Turks, who now ruled Arabia and Egypt and who therefore posed a threat from Red Sea. In 1557, they seized the port of Massawa and the adjacent coast of what is now Eritrea. Two victories by Ethiopians in 1578 and 1589 dislodged them from much of the coast, but Ethiopia's vital sea trade routes remained under threat.

The second threat, also external, came from the arrival with Portuguese soldiers in the country in 1557 of missionaries from the Roman Catholic Jesuit order attempting to convert the Ethiopians from the Coptic to the Roman Catholic faith. The missionaries were so successful that Emperor Susenyos proclaimed the country to be a Roman Catholic nation. This prompted civil war, and in 1632 the proclamation was withdrawn and the emperor was forced to abdicate.

The third great threat was internal. From about 1540 the Cushitic Oromo (or Galla) people began to migrate from what is now southern Ethiopia. They moved north and east into the Hara, Shoa, and Afar regions, driving the Ethiopians north and cutting off their trade routes to the Gulf of Aden. Many Oromo converted to Islam and accepted leadership from the Muslim ruler of Hara, a province in which they became powerful. By 1563 they controlled about one third of the country. After 1600, the Oromo began raiding southwards, reaching Malindi in Kenya by 1699.

An official reception (left)
Seltan Sagad Susenyos, the emperor of Ethiopia from 1607–1632, is shown here greeting Patriarch Mendes, a high-ranking member of the Jesuit religious order.

After the abdication of Susenyos, his son, Fasiladas (1632–1667) restored the Coptic church, expelled the Jesuits, and moved the capital of the empire to Gonder, just north of Lake Tana. Gonder Ethiopia then enjoyed an artistic renaissance, with art and architecture flourishing and many new churches, monasteries, castles, and palaces being built, many under imperial patronage. This renaissance lasted for a century, but during the 18th century the monarchy declined in importance, and increasingly powerful nobles fought among themselves.

In 1788 an Oromo chief, Ali, founded the independent kingdom of Begemder in central and northwest Ethiopia. Other Oromo chiefs set up their own kingdoms in central and southwest Ethiopia, while the nobility increasingly ran its own lands as private fiefdoms.

By the early 1800s, Ethiopia had fallen apart. Ethiopian authors call this period the era of the *Masafent*, or judges for, as in *Old Testament* times:

> *"there was no king …; every man did that which was right in his own eyes."*

Ethiopian decline	
c.1540	Oromo migration begins
1557	Jesuit missionaries arrive in Ethiopia
1578, 1589	Ethiopians defeat Ottoman Turks in Eritrea
1626–1632	Emperor Susenyos proclaims Ethiopia Roman Catholic
1632	Gonder Ethiopia enjoys an artistic renaissance
1633	Jesuits expelled from the country
1700s	Ethiopia begins to decline
1788	Kingdom of Begemder founded
1800s	Ethiopia falls apart as Oromo chiefs break away

Fasiladas Castle, Gonder
After the abdication of Emperor Susneyos, his son, Fasiladas, founded his capital at Gonder where he had the first of several castles built rather than following the then prevailing tradition of moving camps.

Sheik Hussein's tomb
Hussein, an Oromo chief, was an ancient miracle-worker whose tomb was frequently visited by people hoping to benefit from its healing powers. In this illustration it is covered in cloths in to mark a celebration.

© DIAGRAM

39

The Falasha

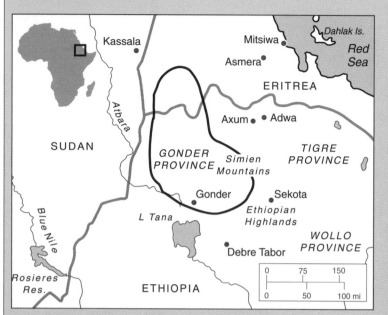

Where they live (above)
The Falasha live around the town of Gonder in the Ethiopian Highlands which surround Lake Tana.

Falasha priests (below)
Two priests (or *cahenet*) read a prayer book in a synagogue (or *mesgid*), a Jewish house of worship. Traditionally, they are required to cover their heads.

The Falasha are Jews who live in the Ethiopian province of Gonder, in the highlands north of Lake Tana. The word Falasha is probably derived from an ancient Ethiopian word meaning "exiles" or "strangers." The Falasha refer to themselves as Beta Israel (House of Israel) and consider Falasha to be an insulting name, although those who use it imply no derogatory meaning.

History
The origins of the Falasha are lost in antiquity, but the people themselves trace their ancestry back to the Jewish bodyguard of the legendary founder of Ethiopia, Menelik I, son of King Solomon and the Queen of Sheba. Other theories suggest that Egyptian or Palestinian Jews escaping religious purges more than 2,000 years ago fled south to settle in Ethiopia, or that Jewish traders in the Red Sea converted the Agau people to Judaism, or that the Falashas might even be the lost tribe of Dan. Whatever their origins, records mention Jews in Ethiopia as early as 200 BCE and Judaism was widespread in the area by the fourth century CE.

The Falasha were often influential in Ethiopia and had long periods of independence and power. Around 960, under the leadership of Queen Esato (Judith), they rebelled against the Axumite kingdom. Under the succeeding Zagwe dynasty they enjoyed great influence, but were subsequently persecuted. Emperor Sarsa-Dengal of Ethiopia (1563–1597) waged a terrible war against them; his successor, Susenyos, broke their resistance in a massacre in 1616. Their numbers, once in the hundreds of thousands, then declined dramatically as a result of persecution or conversion to Christianity.

In the 19th century, missionaries presenting

A royal visit (right)
This is an Ethiopian portrayal of the visit of the Queen of Sheba, accompanied by numerous followers bearing gifts of spices, gold and precious stones, to the court of King Solomon.

themselves as *"White Falasha"* told the Falasha that the promised Messiah had already lived in Jerusalem in an attempt to convert them to Christianity. In 1862 many set out to walk to Palestine to see for themselves. Decimated by disease and starvation, many died and the trek was abandoned at Axum. By the end of the century, only a few thousand Falasha survived in their homeland.

Modern life

After the foundation of the Jewish state of Israel in 1948, considerable debate raged about whether the Falasha were true Jews and thus had the right to Israeli citizenship. In 1975 this right was agreed, and as the Ethiopian civil war intensified, 6,000 Falasha who had fled to safety in neighboring Sudan were taken to Israel between 1979 and 1984. Over the next year, the secret Operation Moses airlifted out another 7,000 refugees from camps in Sudan. At first, the Falasha were given a great welcome, but integration into Israeli society has been slow; in 1996 the "Black Jews" demonstrated in the streets claiming they were treated as second-class citizens. Today, there are less than 800 Falasha left in Ethiopia; 65,000 live in Israel.

Military service (right)
Despite difficulties in integration with Israeli society, the Falasha have had success in adapting to the military requirements of Israeli citizenship.

The history of the Falasha	
300s CE	Judaism well established in Ethiopia
c.960	Falasha rebel against Axumite rule
c.1450	Falasha lands annexed by Ethiopian empire
1616	Massacre of Falasha by Ethiopians
1790s	Existence of Falasha first known in Europe
1862	Aborted trek to Israel
1974	Ethiopian civil war starts; Falasha flee to safety in Sudan and then to Israel
1984–1985	Operation Moses airlifts out 7,000 Falasha
1996	Falasha protest discrimination in Israel
2002	2,000 further Falasha emigrate to Israel

The Somalis

At the time of ancient Egypt, the Somali coast formed part of the region known as Punt, prized by Egyptians for its myrrh trees and such exotic products as gold, ivory, and ebony. Queen Hatshepsut of Egypt (reigned 1473–1458 BCE) sent a massive expedition down the Red Sea to make official contact with this semi-mythical land, although Egyptian merchants had probably been trading with Punt for at least 1,000 years before.

The origin of the modern-day Somalis is uncertain, but by 750 CE what is now Somalia was home to Cushitic people who migrated into the region from the southwest. Arab and Persian traders began to trade with these new inhabitants and to settle on the coast, leading to the capture by Omani Arabs of the port of Mogadishu in 920. Through marriage and cultural and commercial ties between the Cushites and the various Arab and Persian traders, a distinctive Somali people gradually emerged. With the traders came Islam, and during the 1000s, the Somalis had all converted to become Muslims. During this period, the distinctive Somali clan-families originated; their founding fathers, according to tradition, were all related to the Prophet Muhammad and came from Arabia.

Hatshepsut
In this illustration, Hatshepsut is shown wearing the distinctive crown of Upper Egypt bearing the cobra goddess. She was supposed to be the regent for her young stepson, but she assumed control of the government and eventually ruled Egypt for 20 years.

The history of the Somalis

1460s BCE	Queen Hatshepsut of Egypt sends a massive expedition to Punt
750 CE	Cushitic Somalis settle in the region
920	Omani Arabs capture Mogadishu
1000s	Somalis convert to Islam
1200s	Mogadishu becomes most prosperous Somali city-state
1285	Somali state of Ifat established
1328	Ifat becomes a tributary state of Ethiopia
1415	Ifat annexed by Ethiopia
1400s	Somali state of Adal founded
1526–1543	Adal Somalis conquer Ethiopia during reign of Ahmed Gran
1530s	Somalis conquer Ogaden region
1543	Adal annexed by Ethiopia

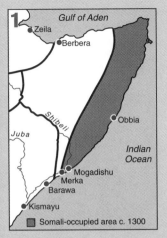

1

Gulf of Aden

Zeila
Berbera
Shibeli
Juba
Obbia
Indian Ocean
Mogadishu
Merka
Barawa
Kismayu

☐ Somali-occupied area c. 1300

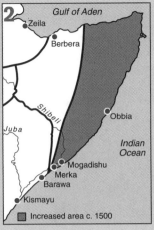

2

Gulf of Aden

Zeila
Berbera
Shibeli
Juba
Obbia
Indian Ocean
Mogadishu
Merka
Barawa
Kismayu

☐ Increased area c. 1500

3

Gulf of Aden

Zeila
Berbera
Shibeli
Juba
Obbia
Indian Ocean
Mogadishu
Merka
Barawa
Kismayu

☐ Increased area c. 1530

4

Gulf of Aden

Zeila
Berbera
Harar
Shibeli
Juba
Obbia
Indian Ocean
Mogadishu
Merka
Barawa
Kismayu

☐ Somali-occupied area c. 1600

0   100   300 km
0   100   200 mi

An expanding kingdom
These four maps show the increasing extent of the
Somali kingdom at the following times: **1** 1300;
2 c.1500; **3** c.1530; and **4** c.1600.

Somali expansion
*At first the Somalis only occupied the Indian Ocean
coastline and the very tip of the Horn of Africa, but
in 1285 a group of small Somali sheikdoms in the
west of the region at the end of the Gulf of Aden
united to establish Ifat. It was soon challenged by
Ethiopia and, in 1328, became a tributary state of
the Empire. After continual rebellion, it was annexed
by Ethiopia in 1415.*

*In the early 1400s, a new united Somali kingdom
of Adal emerged east of Ifat; like Ifat, it too was a
federation of sheikdoms. Under Ahmed Gran
(reigned 1506–1543), Adal then conquered most of
Ethiopia. With the help of Portuguese Christian
troops from Europe, the Ethiopians defeated and
killed Ahmed Gran in battle in 1543, bringing to
an end Somali expansion in the region and
annexing Adal. By this time, however, the Somalis
had consolidated their hold along the Gulf of Aden
and had expanded west into the Ogaden region,
finally expelling its Oromo population during the
1530s, and south along the Indian Ocean.*

Somali boy and camel
As camels have the
ability to survive for
long periods of time
without food or
water, they are vital
to the Somalis in
their semidesert
environment for
transporting
personal
possessions and
goods.

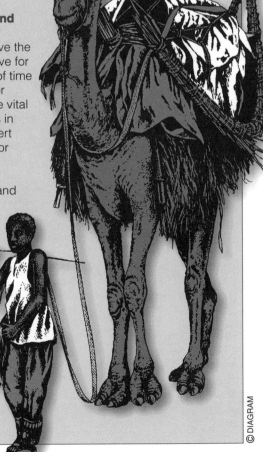

© DIAGRAM

43

COASTAL STATES AND TRADE

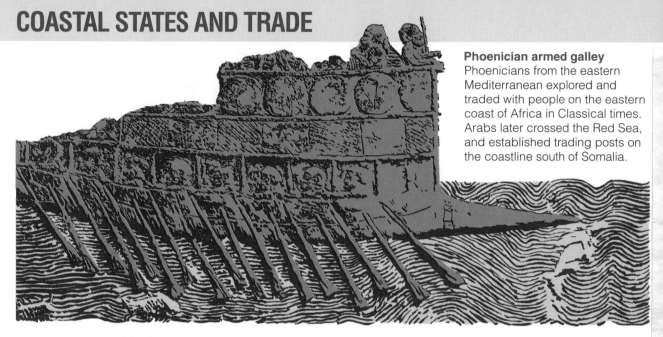

Phoenician armed galley
Phoenicians from the eastern Mediterranean explored and traded with people on the eastern coast of Africa in Classical times. Arabs later crossed the Red Sea, and established trading posts on the coastline south of Somalia.

Trading on the East African coast
This map shows the areas occupied by the Barber and Zanj peoples in the ninth century when Arab geographers divided the East African coast into zones. The Berbers roughly occupied modern-day Somalia, and the Zanj modern-day Kenya and Tanzania. Arab merchants also established trading posts on inshore islands, such as Kilwa, and on the mainland at places, such as Manda, near Lamu in Kenya.

The earliest written accounts of the East African coast appear in *Periplus Maris Ereythraei*, written by a Greek merchant living in Egypt at the end of the first century CE and in the Greek–Egyptian geographer Ptolemy's *Geography*, written a century later.

The *Periplus* describes the Somali coastline, its six or so trading ports, and the fact that customs were charged on ships rounding Cape Guardafui at the very tip of the Horn of Africa. It also records ships sailing to western India and returning laden with cotton, grain, oil, and sugar, while others traded up into the Red Sea, taking aromatic gums, ivory, tortoiseshell, and slaves in return for copper, tin, and fine cloth.

Ptolemy provides a more detailed geographical account of the coastline, again discussing Somalia. The discovery of Greek and Roman coins in East Africa, as well as accounts of migration to the area, all suggest that contacts between the Classical World and East Africa were not by any means unusual.

Arab contacts

The most frequent visitors to East Africa were Arab traders, who took advantage of the prevailing winds in the winter months to arrive with the northeast monsoon, returning in the summer with the southwest winds. They preferred the coastline south of Somalia because of its wetter climate, sheltered anchorages, and more easily defended offshore islands. They named this coast Azania, or Land of Zanj, that is the land of black people. By 500 CE, the area was inhabited by Bantu-speaking peoples, but little is known about Azania until the ninth century, as no settlements have been found predating this period.

Arab geographers of the time divided the East African coast into four distinct zones: Berber, roughly modern-day Somalia; Zanj, which is Kenya and Tanzania; Sofala, or Mozambique, which was shipping out gold by the 10th century; and an ill-defined Waq waq. The only island described is Pemba, north of Zanzibar.

The Arab merchants who traded with East Africa established their trading posts mainly on the offshore islands, notably Pemba, and on inshore islands like Kilwa, on the southern Tanzania coast, because such islands provided greater security from attacks from the mainland. They did, however, develop settlements on the mainland, such as Mogadishu in Somalia and Manda, near Lamu in Kenya. Most of the settlers came from the Persian Gulf, notably Siraf and Bahrain, although some possibly came from the mouth of the Indus River in northwest India.

The buildings at Manda date from around the ninth century and are protected by seawalls of coral blocks each weighing up to one ton each. At both Manda and Kilwa, however, most buildings were of wattle and daub, although some later ones were built of stone. Both Manda and Kilwa had considerable Bantu iron-smelting industries already established, which helped the Arabs to develop the ports.

The people of Kilwa used a local currency of cowrie shells and traded with merchants from the Persian Gulf. Glass beads were imported from India and porcelain arrived from China via India or the Persian Gulf. Trade was also conducted with the large offshore island of Madagascar. At Manda, most trade was by barter; with ivory exported in return for Islamic pottery and, in the 9th and 10th centuries, Chinese porcelain.

Tribute to a sultan (below)
These two copper coins, dating from the 14th century, are inscribed with the name of one of the sultans of Kilwa.

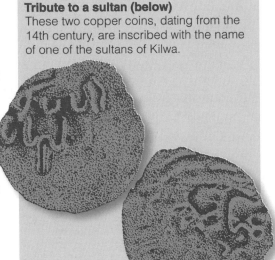

Influence from abroad (below)
This door, discovered at Fort Jesus, Lamu, Kenya, displays distinctive Arabic craftsmanship in its decorative features.

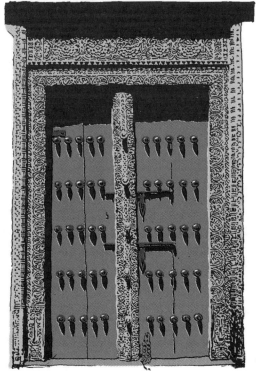

©DIAGRAM

Swahili culture and history

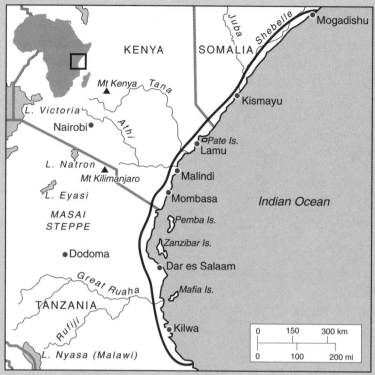

Where the Swahili lived
This map shows the area of East Africa occupied by the Swahili people. It stretched from Mogadishu in the north to Kilwa in the south. By the 1100s a distinct Swahili culture existed and, c.1400, Kilwa had become the most important trading center on the east coast of Africa.

Clay pots
Metalworkers melted copper in clay pots, such as those illustrated below, during what is known as the golden age of Swahili culture, which lasted from c.1200–1500 CE.

The Swahili live in the coastal region and on the small offshore islands of Tanzania, Kenya, and Somalia. Their name is derived from the Arabic word sawahil, meaning "coast dwellers." Today, they number approximately 1 million, although their language is spoken by millions of people, and is the official language of both Kenya and Tanzania.

The Swahili people are of mixed Black African, Arab, and Persian descent. The coastal Black Africans were mainly Bantu and Cushitic groups who had migrated into the area from the northwest, and some Bantu from the south, before 1000 CE. After the Bantu-speaking people came Muslim Arabs and other people from southwest Asia, initially from Oman and Persia and later from Yemen and Arabia. Most were attracted by the prospect of profiting from the trade in ivory, skins, and slaves, although some were seeking refuge from political or religious persecution.

By the start of the second millennium, there were Arab settlements in – from north to south – the ports of Mogadishu, Lamu, Malindi, Zanzibar, and Kilwa. Arabs ruled some of these settlements, Africans others. Around 1200 CE, Persians from Shiraz established the Shirazi dynasty on the Banadir coast around Mogadishu.

Swahili dominance

By the 1100s, a distinct Swahili people and culture had emerged from the intermingling, mainly through marriage and trade, of these Arab, African, and Persian groups.

The Swahilis set up a number of small kingdoms based on the existing trading cities up and down the coast. One of the most important was Kilwa. Here gold, gum, ivory, slaves, and lumber from inland were traded for cotton, glass, porcelain, and pottery, supplied by Arabian, Chinese, and Indian merchants. Kilwa was just one of about 40 such trading ports along the East African coast and on the islands of Pemba and Zanzibar. Ruins of mosques and palaces still survive in many places.

This golden age of Swahili dominance came to an abrupt halt with the arrival of Portuguese adventurers on the coast in 1498, ending Swahili independence by 1509. During the 17th century, Omani Arab traders settled on the coast, driving out the Portuguese and making the coastline part of the Omani empire. Swahili dominance of the coastline was now over.

Blowing his *siwa* (right)
A Swahilli man from Lamu announces a religious ceremony with the use of a traditional brass horn, probably made in the 18th century.

Remnants of a culture (above)
Ruins have been found at many places in East Africa which bear witness to the splendour of the Swahili civilization. These ruins were found at Gedi, Kenya.

M*ankala* board (right)
This board was made by a Swahili craftsman in Tanzania. The game *mankala* has been played for at least 7,000 years, and versions of it can be found throughout Africa as well as the rest of the world.

Grandee's chair (above)
Elaborately carved in ebony and ivory, such chairs as this would have been offered as a sign of respect to visiting notables from 1300s–1800s.

© DIAGRAM

47

Indian Ocean trade

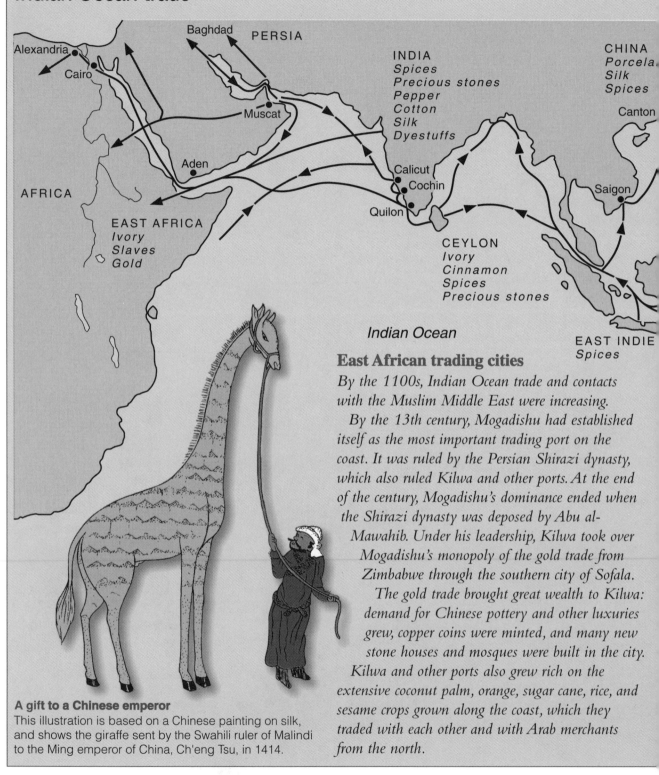

Baghdad

PERSIA

Alexandria

Cairo

INDIA
Spices
Precious stones
Pepper
Cotton
Silk
Dyestuffs

CHINA
Porcela...
Silk
Spices

Muscat

Canton

Aden

AFRICA

Calicut
Cochin

Saigon

Quilon

EAST AFRICA
Ivory
Slaves
Gold

CEYLON
Ivory
Cinnamon
Spices
Precious stones

Indian Ocean

EAST INDIE...
Spices

East African trading cities

By the 1100s, Indian Ocean trade and contacts with the Muslim Middle East were increasing.

By the 13th century, Mogadishu had established itself as the most important trading port on the coast. It was ruled by the Persian Shirazi dynasty, which also ruled Kilwa and other ports. At the end of the century, Mogadishu's dominance ended when the Shirazi dynasty was deposed by Abu al-Mawahib. Under his leadership, Kilwa took over Mogadishu's monopoly of the gold trade from Zimbabwe through the southern city of Sofala.

The gold trade brought great wealth to Kilwa: demand for Chinese pottery and other luxuries grew, copper coins were minted, and many new stone houses and mosques were built in the city. Kilwa and other ports also grew rich on the extensive coconut palm, orange, sugar cane, rice, and sesame crops grown along the coast, which they traded with each other and with Arab merchants from the north.

A gift to a Chinese emperor
This illustration is based on a Chinese painting on silk, and shows the giraffe sent by the Swahili ruler of Malindi to the Ming emperor of China, Ch'eng Tsu, in 1414.

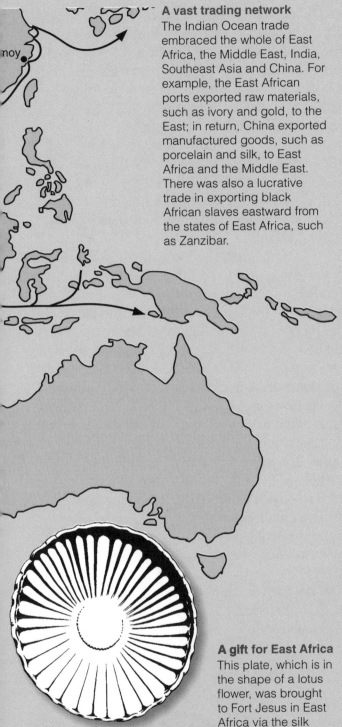

A vast trading network
The Indian Ocean trade embraced the whole of East Africa, the Middle East, India, Southeast Asia and China. For example, the East African ports exported raw materials, such as ivory and gold, to the East; in return, China exported manufactured goods, such as porcelain and silk, to East Africa and the Middle East. There was also a lucrative trade in exporting black African slaves eastward from the states of East Africa, such as Zanzibar.

A gift for East Africa
This plate, which is in the shape of a lotus flower, was brought to Fort Jesus in East Africa via the silk routes.

Throughout the 14th and 15th centuries, the rival ports of East Africa vied for dominance with Kilwa. Mombasa, Malindi, and Mogadishu all enjoyed periods of great wealth. Each of these city-states was independent and had its own character and ruler. The ruling class of these states comprised Swahilis and Muslims, most of whome were merchants. Further down the social scale was a laboring class of Black African slaves, and transient Arabs.

Islamic East Africa

Despite their location, the main influence in each city was Islamic rather than African, and each was bound by the sea to a distant Islamic civilization and trading network. Gold, copper, minerals, and other raw materials, as well as exotic products such as rhinoceros horns, amber, leopard skins, and ivory flowed down to the coastal cities, where they were traded in exchange for cloth, beads and manufactured goods, most of which came from the Arab world, India, and China.

The scale of this Indian Ocean trade network was vast, encompassing the whole of East Africa, the Middle East, India, Southeast Asia, and China. The East African ports exported raw materials and precious commodities from the interior, while Asia exported manufactured goods, such as daggers, ironware, glass, and silk. Arabs and Persians dominated the seaborne trade in the western Indian Ocean, while the Chinese dominated the eastern Indian Ocean. The timescale of this trade was long, however, because goods were usually shipped from one port to the next, where they were unloaded, sold on, and then reloaded into another ship for transport to the next port. However, this trade did bring considerable wealth to East Africa and to all those who took part in it.

Portuguese and Omani rule

Coastal states in East Africa

1000 BCE–1000 CE	Bantus and Cushites migrate into East Africa
900s	Arab trading posts set up at Mogadishu and Kilwa
1100s	Distinctive Swahili people and culture exists
1107	Mosque built in Zanzibar
c.1150	Mombasa and Malindi founded
1200s	Mogadishu at height of its power
c.1250	Persian Shirazi dynasty founded near Mogadishu
1400s	Kilwa establishes itself as most important Swahili city on coast
c.1470	Mombasa begins to eclipse Kilwa
1498	Portuguese navigator Vasco da Gama arrives on the coast
1502–1509	Portuguese conquer East African coast to control trade
1652	Omanis sack Zanzibar and Pate
1698	Omanis conquer much of coast
1822–1837	East Africa becomes part of Sultanate of Oman
1840	Omani capital moved from Muscat to Zanzibar

In 1498 the Portuguese navigator Vasco da Gama visited East Africa on his way to India. The Portuguese were looking for a route to India and the Far East of Asia to gain access to the lucrative trade in spices. For this, they needed supply bases and forts along the coast and control over the trading city-states of East Africa.

The Portuguese first attacked in 1502, when they bombarded Kilwa. They captured the city in 1505 and then went on to sack Mombasa. By 1509 they controlled all the coastal cities apart from Mogadishu. In this campaign, they were helped not just by their technological and military superiority but also by local allies, notably Malindi, a long-term rival of Mombasa. The Portuguese based themselves on the offshore islands of Pemba and Zanzibar and rebuilt and strengthened forts at Kilwa and elsewhere.

Opposition to the Portuguese came from the Ottoman Turks, who by now were the dominant Muslim power in the Middle East and North Africa. In 1585, and again in 1588, Turkish expeditions sailed south from Somalia and encouraged the coastal cities to revolt but they were met by Portuguese fleets sent from its Indian colony of Goa. A further threat came from Mombasa, which rose in revolt in 1589. In retaliation, the Portuguese sacked the city for the third time, bringing its independence to an end.

For the whole of the 17th century, the Portuguese dominated East Africa and its trade from their new base at Mombasa. Their main interest was economic, not imperial. They opened customs houses at Mombasa and Pate to collect dues, developed the local trade in timber, rice, pitch, and cereals, and

A Portuguese carrack (below)
Such ships were used by early European explorers of the East African coast.

Seyyid Said (right)
An illustration based on a contemporary view of a sultan of Zanzibar.

exported ivory, gold, amber, and coral in return for ironware, weapons, beads, cotton, silks, and spices.

Omani domination

The Portuguese were not invulnerable, however. Union with Spain between 1580 and 1640, and commercial competition with Holland and England, weakened their control over East Africa and the Indian Ocean. In 1650 they lost the strategic port of Muscat, at the entrance to the Persian Gulf, to the eastern Arabian state of Oman; two years later the Omanis sacked Zanzibar and Pate and murdered their Portuguese inhabitants. Over the next 50 years, the Omanis increased their presence in East Africa, capturing Mombasa in 1698 and ending the Portuguese presence on the coast.

Although their influence grew during the 18th century, the Omanis never fully controlled East Africa. There was much rivalry between the city-states, dynastic struggles among the Omanis themselves, and constant rebellion against Omani rule. As a result, the Omanis brought the entire coastline under their control between 1822 and 1837. In 1840 Sultan Seyyid Said consolidated this control by moving the capital of his empire from Muscat to Zanzibar itself. By the time of his death in 1856, Zanzibar had become one of the largest trading ports in the Indian Ocean and a center of international trade.

The *gereza* on Kilwa (below)
This fortress was built by the Portuguese in the 16th century. Their arrival on the coast of East Africa brought the Arab and Swahili dominance of trade there to an end.

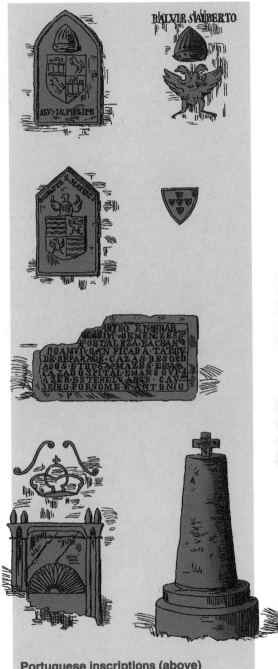

Portuguese inscriptions (above)
These inscriptions, which were found in the ruins of various buildings found at Mombasa, Makupa, and Melinde, recall the extent of Portuguese influence in East Africa during the 16th century.

© DIAGRAM

BETWEEN THE LAKES

At the court of Mutesa I (right)
The British explorers John Hanning Speke and James Augustus Grant visited Buganda in the 1860s during their search for the source of the Nile. This illustration shows the welcome they received upon their arrival.

Mutesa I (above)
He became *kabaka* (king) of Buganda in 1856, and made contact with the first European explorers in the 1870s.

An expanding kingdom (below)
The Ganda people first settled near Lake Victoria around 1000 CE. Over the centuries they considerably expanded their influence. These maps show the extent of the kingdom at the following times: **1** 16th century; **2** 17th century; **3** 18th century; **4** 19th century.

The peoples who live between the Great Lakes are Bantu speakers who arrived in the region from the Congo basin by about 1000 CE. The two main peoples are the Ganda, who founded Buganda, and the Nyoro, who founded Bunyoro. Together these two kingdoms formed the basis of the modern-day state of Uganda.

Buganda

Knowledge about the early history of Buganda and the Ganda people is plentiful, as each clan kept its own oral history while court historians preserved royal accounts. The first Ganda to arrive in the region settled on the northwest corner of Lake Victoria around the Kyadondo region. By the 14th century, this became the heart of the Buganda kingdom.

16th century

17th century

18th century

19th century

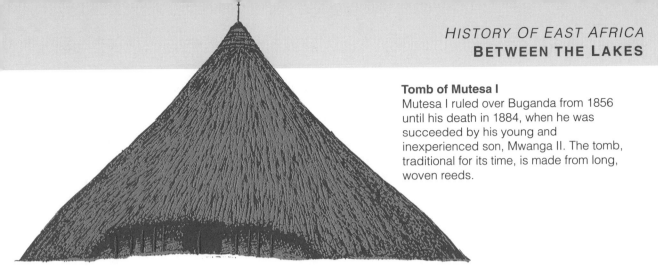

Tomb of Mutesa I
Mutesa I ruled over Buganda from 1856 until his death in 1884, when he was succeeded by his young and inexperienced son, Mwanga II. The tomb, traditional for its time, is made from long, woven reeds.

The head of state of Buganda was the *kabaka*, whose role initially was one of arbiter rather than ruler. His power was limited by that of the *batakas*, or clan heads. During the 18th century, however, successive *kabakas* skilfully increased their powers at the expense of the *batakas*. Buganda eventually became a centralized monarchy with the *kabaka* acting as king.

The kingdom benefited from a highly organized system of government, led by the *kabaka* with help from his *Lukiko* (council of ministers). Prestige, wealth, and status were achieved through military service or service at the court of the *kabaka*. The *kabaka* guaranteed the rights of all his subjects wherever they resided, land was plentiful, and people were not dependent on their families or neighbors for their status and security.

Buganda was a wealthy trading nation with a currency of cowrie shells, their value denoted by the holes drilled in the shells so that they could be suspended on strings. The Basese, who are related to the Ganda and live on the islands in Lake Victoria, provided the *kabakas* with a navy and could sometimes muster fleets of as many as 100 vessels, each crewed by up to 30 men.

From the 16th century onward, Buganda steadily increased in size, but its growing economic, political, and military strength led to tension and sometimes conflict with its neighbors, notably the dominant Bunyoro to its north. By the mid-19th century, Buganda had supplanted Bunyoro in importance. Its military superiority, a talent for administration, and strong leadership made it the most important state in the region.

Mutesa II
The last of a dynasty, Mutesa II became *kabaka* (king) of Buganda in 1939 and, in 1963, the first president of the Republic of Uganda. Although he ruled over Buganda from 1939–1966, the kingdom was never fully independent under his control as it remained a province of the British Uganda Protectorate until1962.

© DIAGRAM

53

Bunyoro kingdom

The historic kingdom of Bunyoro was founded by the Bantu-speaking Nyoro, or Banyoro people, of northwest Uganda. Nyoro history is centered around the empire of Bunyoro-Kitara and later the Bunyoro kingdom.

Oral history attributes the founding of the first Bunyoro-Kitara empire to the mythical Abatembuzi (or Tembuzi) people. They were succeeded by the Bachwezi (or Chwezi) dynasty (c.1350–1500 CE) about whom little is certain except that they were an immigrant, cattle-herding people. The Bachwezi established a centralized monarchy over the local Bantu peoples. They had a hierarchy of officials and also maintained an army.

After the death of the last Bachwezi *bakama* (king), Wamara, in c.1500, the Bunyoro-Kitara empire broke up into several small states, one of which was Bunyoro. The Babito dynasty then took control of Bunyoro. The Babito were originally Lwo-speaking River-Lake Nilotes peoples who migrated from the Nile River in present-day southern Sudan to the lakes region of modern Uganda. Under their first *omukama* (ruler), Mpuga Rukidi, the Babito kept many of the previous dynasty's rituals and customs, although they were never able to match its power or influence in the region. Raids against neighboring peoples expanded Bunyoro so that, by 1870, it extended to the north and east of the Nile and to the west of Lake Victoria.

Bunyoro was governed as a loose federation of *saza*

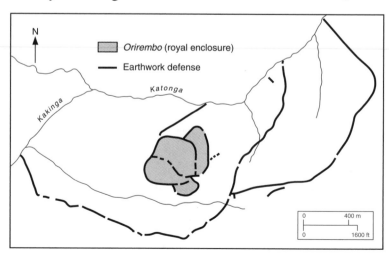

Earthworks
This earthwork, constructed by the Bachwezi, was made as a defense against the southern border of Bunyoro-Kitara. It was situated at Biggo in the district of Bwera,Uganda. The system of trenches and ditches protected large herds of cattle. An *orirembo*, or royal enclosure, also formed part of the earthwork.

Royal appearance
Accompanied by his retinue, an *omukama*, or ruler of Bunyoro, leaves his royal palace.

(provinces), each under a chief appointed by the *omukama*. These *saza* were semi-independent and some on the edge of Bunyoro territory broke away to form independent states. During the long reign of *Omukama* Kyebambe Nyamutukura III (1786–1835), for instance, four of his sons turned against him. One of them, Kaboyo Omuhanwa, took the *saza* of Toro and, in c.1830, established his own kingdom. Toro then became one of the border regions in dispute between the various Nyoro factions and fought a lengthy war with Bunyoro between 1859–1870.

Omukama Kabalega (reigned 1870–1898) tried to unite Bunyoro once again and regain the ascendancy it had lost on the rise of Buganda, to its southeast. Kabalega created the *Abarusura*, a standing army of 20,000 men in ten divisions, each with its own commander. One division went to the capital Masindi to maintain law and order, under Kabalega's greatest general, Rwabudongo, while others raided rebel provinces like Toro. His policy was only a partial success, as Bunyoro was never again to regain its former glory.

An empire at the height of its powers
This map shows the empire of Bunyoro-Kitara in the early 16th century, a short time before its disintegration. The most important empire to emerge from the break-up was Bunyoro.

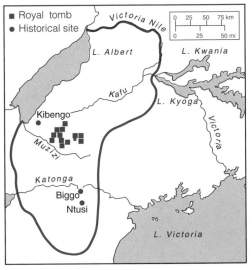

©DIAGRAM

Ruanda-Urundi

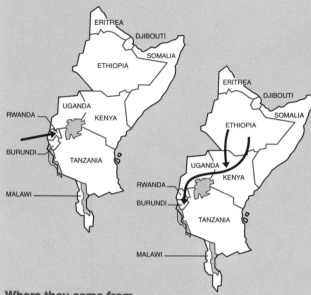

Where they came from
The Tutsi originated from the north (modern Ethiopia), whereas the Hutu came from the west (modern Congo), into the modern-day states of Rwanda and Burundi.

Tutsi dancer
A typical dancer would wear a headdress to accentuate the rhythmic movements of the dance, a leopardskin cloak, and also carry a javelin-like wand.

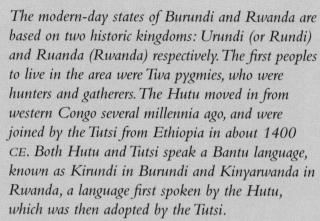

The modern-day states of Burundi and Rwanda are based on two historic kingdoms: Urundi (or Rundi) and Ruanda (Rwanda) respectively. The first peoples to live in the area were Twa pygmies, who were hunters and gatherers. The Hutu moved in from western Congo several millennia ago, and were joined by the Tutsi from Ethiopia in about 1400 CE. Both Hutu and Tutsi speak a Bantu language, known as Kirundi in Burundi and Kinyarwanda in Rwanda, a language first spoken by the Hutu, which was then adopted by the Tutsi.

The Tutsi soon dominated the Hutu, making them virtual slaves. In the 16th century, the Tutsi established the kingdom of Ruanda, causing the rulers of the neighboring Bunyoro kingdom to launch a series of attacks on the new state, uniting Tutsi and Hutu against them. The Tutsi rulers

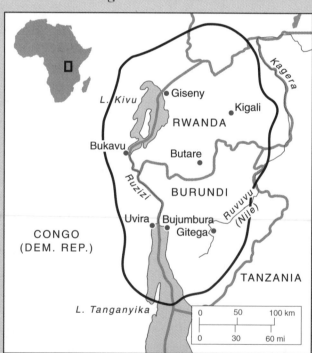

Two ethnic groups
This map shows the area in East Africa currently occupied by the Hutu and Tutsi people, who make up the majority ethnic groups of Burundi and Rwanda.

(known as nyiginya*) claimed descent from the supreme being, Imana. The origins of the Urundi kingdom are less certain, but it emerged with similar institutions and practices as Ruanda.*

During the next two centuries, both kingdoms expanded their territories, establishing centralized and stable realms governed by officials. Each kingdom was ruled by a Tutsi king, called the mwami *(plural* bami*). The cattle-owning minority Tutsi formed the aristocracy in both kingdoms, with the Hutu making up the often-exploited majority.*

During the 19th century, Ruanda emerged as one of the most powerful states in the region, challenged only by Bunyoro.

Victim of retaliation
Following an unsuccessful revolt by the Hutu in 1972, the Tutsi killed over 100,000 Hutu people in Burundi. This illustration depicts one of the survivors being looked after by a medical orderly caught up in the conflict.

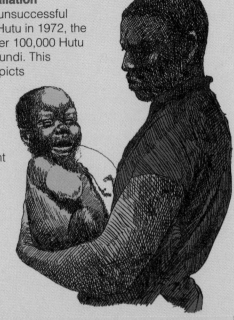

Headdresses
The flowing headdress of a Tutsi king is shown (left). Beneath the hair is a broad head-band, decorated with beadwork, and underneath this band are added beaded tassells which hang over the face of the ruler. The headdress (below), a variation on the same theme, is worn by some Tutsi women of royal descent.

57

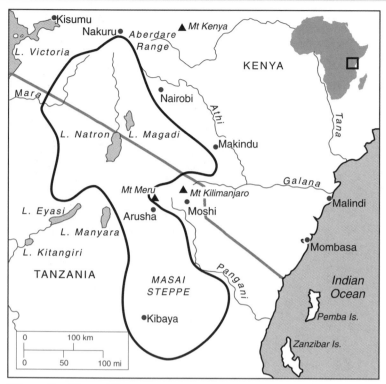

Where the Maasai live
This map shows the modern extent of the Maasai, a collection of groups who live in the grasslands of the Great Rift Valley that straddle the border of Kenya and Tanzania.

Maasai shields
Made from buffalo hide, and weighing up to 50lb (23 kg) each, these shields carry designs called *sirata* that indicate the age group and family of their owners.

Orinkas
These are ceremonial clubs carried by men to age group meetings. They were formerly made from ivory or rhinoceros horn, but the use of these materials is now illegal.

The great plains of the Eastern Highlands occupy much of present-day Kenya, Tanzania, and Uganda. They stretch from the coastal region in the east across to the western branch of the Rift Valley system, although the plains themselves are almost cut in two distinct halves by the Great Rift Valley itself. The vast majority of people who settled on these plains are Highland-Plain Nilotes, including the Maasai and Karamojong, although some, like the Kikuyu, are Bantu-speakers.

The Maasai

The Maasai are a collection of Highland-Plain Nilotes who live mostly in the grassy plains of Kenya and Tanzania. The pastoral Maasai are often seen as the proper Maasai, but other Maasai peoples include the Samburu of Kenya and the Arusha of Tanzania. The current population is 250,000 in total.

The Maasai peoples originally came from the south-western fringe of the Ethiopian Highlands, and migrated south to the plains of East Africa some time between

Ready to fight
This lineup shows a group of young Maasai warriors in full battle attire. The feathered headdresses were worn to make it more difficult for the enemy to count their numbers.

1000 to 1500 CE. They settled initially to the east of the Great Rift Valley between mounts Kilimanjaro and Kenya. From the 1600s, the Maasai and the Arusha then migrated southward while the Samburu turned west and settled in the mountain pastures.

The 18th century was a period of increasing power and geographical expansion for the Maasai. Despite their relatively small numbers, by the early 19th century they dominated the region between Mount Elgon and Mount Kenya in the north and Dodoma, central Tanzania, in the south. As a rule, they were not conquerors, but came into conflict with their neighbors or other Maasai groups when raiding cattle or defending their own herds.

However, the 19th century was a period of increasingly frequent civil wars among the Maasai. In particular, the pastoral Maasai – united for the first time under one leader, the *laibon* (prophet) Mbatiany – were in conflict with the *Laikipiak*, or agricultural Maasai. This was followed by the onset of *rinderpest* (a cattle disease) which decimated their herds, smallpox and cholera epidemics, and, during the 1880s and 1890s, famine, a period known as *Ol Matai*, "the time of *rinderpest* and famine." Thousands of Maasai died or were impoverished, leading to further civil wars which took place at the turn of the century.

Mark of prestige
Graduate warriors, or *elmoran*, wore ornate headdresses made from ostrich feathers.

© DIAGRAM

59

The Karamojong and the Shambaa

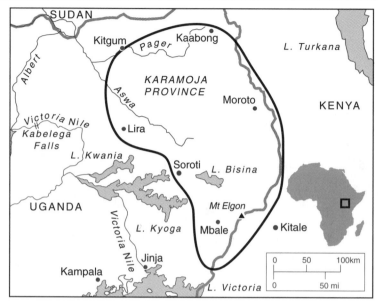

Where they live
This map shows the modern extent of the Karamojong, who live in Karamoja, a semiarid plateau in northeast Uganda.

Karamojong is the collective name given to several closely-related Highland-Plain Nilotes who today live in Karamoja, a semiarid plateau in northeast Uganda on the border with Kenya. The main groups are the Dodoth, Jie, Bokora, Matheniko, and Pian. The Turkana, who live across the border in Kenya, are sometimes considered one of the Karamojong.

The Karamojong moved into Karamoja after 1000 CE. They were originally Nilo-Hamitic in origin; some of their ancestors probably came from North Africa. During the 1700s they settled north of Mount Elgon, but from 1706–1733 endured a period of drought and famine known as the *Nyamciere*. The Karamojong were pastoralists, herding animals in a remote and hostile environment. Cattle rustling was a primary occupation, with one group of Karamojong often raiding the cattle of another. In 1894 drought and an epidemic of cattle disease decimated their herds and led to the dispersal of the Karamojong across Uganda and neighboring Kenya.

Karamojong society was organized into several systems, including the hereditary clan, each of which had its own cattle brand, and the geographical *ngitela,* areas occupied by people who celebrated social and religious events together. Another system was *ngikenoi* – which means "fireplaces with three stones," a name that referred to the Karamojongs' origins – whose members gathered for sacrifices and other ceremonies.

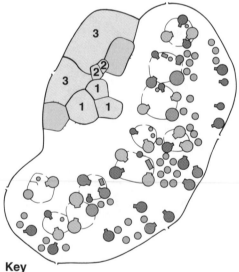

Key
- 🐚 Dwelling house
- ● Storehouse
- ● Grass storage rack
- ● Stilted storehouse (calves kept underneath)
- 🐚 Meeting house used by unmarried women

- ☐ Enclosure:
  1 Goats and sheep
  2 Calves
  3 Cattle
- ☐ Place where cattle are milked

Karamojong village
The composition of a typical Karamojong village is shown in this plan. Most Karamojong are cattle-herding pastoralists who also keep sheep and goats. Men spend most of their time with the herds, and move with the cattle from one grazing ground to another. In the dry season they may be many miles from home, living in makeshift homes. Karamojong women spend most of their time in or near the village, and are expected to do all the hard work including collecting firewood, fetching water and growing and tending the crops.

The Shambaa

The coastal plain of Tanzania is occupied by a cluster of closely related ethnic groups, including the Bondei, Pare, and Shambala, collectively called the Shambaa. Although they are technically known as an Eastern Bantu people, the Shambaa are in fact descended from Bantu and Cushitic ancestors. Around 1200 CE, Bantu speakers migrating into East Africa from Central Africa mingled with Cushitic peoples, who were also moving into the region. Interaction between the two cultures led to the development of the Shambaa and other groups.

At first, the Shambaa's ancestors lived in widespread, independent settlements. However, after experiencing Maasai raids in the early 18th century, the various family-based groups began to form closer political unions. Under their chieftain, Mbegha, the Shambaa began to develop a powerful, centralized state. Ruled by a group known as the Kilindi, the Shambaa kingdom reached its height in the 19th century under King Kimweri ye Nyumbai.

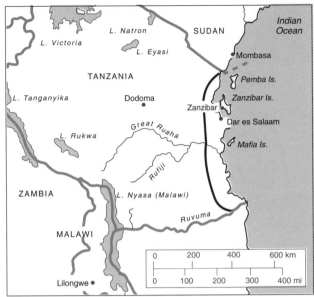

Where they live (above)
This map shows the modern extent of the Shambaa, a cluster of closely-related groups who live on the coastal plain of Tanzania.

***Ankole* cattle (below)**
Men tend to their herds of distinctively long-horned cattle.

© DIAGRAM

61

The Nyamwezi

The Nyamwezi people are one of a number of Bantu-speaking peoples who live in west-central Tanzania. They were originally called Wanyamwezi, "people of the moon," because they came from the west, where the new moon is first seen. Their homeland is known as Unyamwezi. Local traditions hold that the region the Nyamwezi presently live in was uninhabited until the 17th century. Then families began to arrive from various directions. The earliest records are from the late 1600s, and concern the Galagansa, a western group. The Nyamwezi formed a number of self-governing units called *ntemi* (chiefdoms). A few powerful chiefdoms, such as the Ha, Zinza, and Ngoni, dominated the others.

By about 1800 traders from these groups were visiting the east coast, whose inhabitants named them Wanyamwezi. The Nyamwezi gained a considerable reputation as pioneers of long-distance trade in East and Central Africa by organizing trading caravans. The principal trade was in iron, made and worked by the northern Nyamwezi, and salt. Later, copper and ivory became the main commodities, as well as some involvement in slave trading.

During the 1800s the Nyamwezi bought guns and some groups established standing armies. As a result, several wars broke out between the chiefdoms, as well as armed conflicts with the Arab traders from the coast. In 1860 a *ntemi* chief, Mirambo, managed to establish his dominance over several chiefdoms. His empire was short-lived, as it came into conflict with Arab traders and broke up soon after his death in 1884.

Ready for action
Local tribesmen, together with their herd of camels, begin their journey across the arid Tanzanian plain.

Importing goods (above)
This map shows the principal trading route from Zanzibar on the East African coast inland from the 16th to the 19th centuries.

Where they live (above)
This map shows the modern extent of the Nyanwezi, who live in west-central Tanzania.

© DIAGRAM

63

The Kikuyu

A nomadic lifestyle

The Kikuyu came to Kenya from the north and west and began to settle in Kikuyuland in the 1500s. They were originally hunters and nomadic pastoralists (livestock raisers who migrated with their herds).

Where they live

This map shows the modern extent of the Kikuyu, who live in Kikuyuland, a highland plateau which is part of the lush Great Rift Valley at the foot of Mount Kenya.

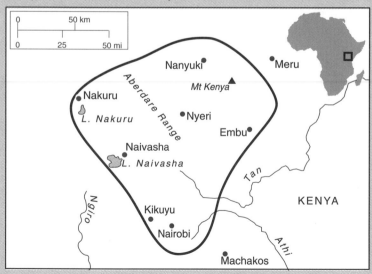

The Kikuyu, sometimes known as the Gikuyu, are the largest ethnic group in Kenya today, totaling more than five million. They live in Kikuyuland, a highland plateau in the Great Rift Valley southeast of Mount Kenya. Their language, also called Kikuyu, is one of the Bantu group of languages, although many also speak Swahili.

The origins of the Kikuyu are obscure. Ethnologists believe that Bantu-speaking people first settled in Kenya in about 1400 CE, although they could have arrived much earlier. The Kikuyu then arrived from the north and west and began to settle in Kikuyuland in the 1500s. They were originally hunters and pastoralists, migrating with their herds. Because land was plentiful, they had no knowledge of, or need for, crop rotation, farming their land until it was exhausted and then moving on to a new patch.

During the next 300 years, they continued to expand their territory, generally keeping on good terms with their Maasai neighbors, with whom they traded their agricultural produce for animal hides and livestock.

Kikuyu society was highly structured, with a strong emphasis on the family. The Kikuyu were divided into two groups, the Maina and Mwangi. In addition, each person also belonged to an age-set, called a riika. Which riika people belonged to depended on the time the boys and girls were first circumcised. The Kikuyu believed that the age-set system helped to bind people together.

Each village was ruled by a council of nine elders. Each group of nine villages elected a representative to a higher council for an area known as mbari, *meaning a ridge; the Kikuyu lived on a plateau full of ridges and valleys. Each* mbari *sent a representative to a district council. The Kikuyu's system of landholding was based on the* mbari. *The councils acted as courts of law when necessary.*

The more senior elders served as high priests in the Kikuyu religion, which was founded on a belief in one all-powerful god called Ngai. According to legend, the Kikuyu are descended from one of Ngai's three sons, Gikuyu, who chose to be a farmer. Gikuyu married a wife provided by Ngai, named Moombi, the creator. She bore him nine daughters, each of whom had a family who became a clan, taking their mother's name.

Ceremonial shields
Shields like these were used by the Kikuyu while dancing at initiation ceremonies to mark various stages in male development. There is no evidence to suggest that they were ever used in warfare.

Overcoming obstacles (above)
A boat is hauled through a mass of matted grass and papyrus from the surrounding swamps during an attempt by European explorers to trace the source of the Nile.

A mission of mercy (above)
John Hanning Speke earnestly tries to save the wife of a chief from execution during one of his expeditions to the African continent.

As we have already seen, the first Europeans to make an impact in East Africa were the Portuguese who, as a result of Vasco da Gama's voyage up the coast of East Africa in 1498, established almost total control over the coastline and its lucrative Indian Ocean trade by 1509. This domination lasted for two centuries.

The main threat to the Portuguese came from the Arabian peninsula to the north, where the trading state of Oman sought to capture the Portuguese trade with India. By 1698 the Omanis had taken Mombasa, ending Portuguese rule over the coast. For the next 150 years, the Omanis were the dominant influence in the region, first based in their capital, Muscat and then, in 1840, from the island of Zanzibar. European contact with the east coast was restricted to trade with its maritime cities.

Exploration and conversion

This situation began to change at the end of the 18th century and the arrival of the first European explorers in the region. Their motives were both geographic and inquisitive. Africa was the last great continent to be explored and the source of many of its rivers – including the Congo in the center and, above all, the Nile in the north – were unknown. In 1768–1773, the Scotsman James Bruce explored the Nile Valley and the Red Sea,

"Dr Livingstone, I presume?"
A 19th-century newspaper shows the meeting in Africa in 1871 between David Livingstone and Henry Morton Stanley.

confirming that Lake Tana in Ethiopia was the source of the Blue Nile, one of its main tributaries.

In 1862 John Hanning Speke, an Englishman, claimed that the source of the main river – the White Nile – was at the Ripon Falls to the north of Lake Victoria. He was correct, although the most distant source is in the Ruwenzori Highlands to the west of Lake Edward.

By this time, the focus of exploration had widened to include both the conversion of the African peoples to Christianity, and their betterment through exposure to European ideals, knowledge, and, of course, trade.

In achieving these goals, more enlightened Europeans also sought to eradicate the curse of slavery from the region, a trade dominated in East Africa by Zanzibar. In 1807 the British had made it illegal for Britons to engage in the slave trade and finally abolished slavery throughout their empire in 1833, seeking also to eradicate it elsewhere in the world.

In this spirit, another Scot, David Livingstone, made three epic journeys between 1841 and his death in 1873, exploring much of the Great Lakes region. At the same time the American Henry Morton Stanley, much more of an adventurer than an explorer, sailed round Lake Victoria and then down the great Congo River to its estuary on the Atlantic coast. Tales of these and other explorers' exploits did much to awaken European interest in what many then still considered to be the "dark continent."

Explorers (with countries represented)

- ┈┈┈ John Speke and James Grant (United Kingdom) 1860–1863
- ▬▬▬ Henry Morton Stanley (US) 1871–1872
- David Livingstone (United Kingdom):
- ▬▬▬ First (missionary) journeys 1841–1856
- ▬ ▬ ▬ Zambezi Expedition 1856–1864
- ┄┄┄ Final Expedition 1866–1873

Exploring East Africa

The map above shows exploration routes followed by the British and Americans, with the first missionary journeys and expeditions, during the period 1849–1873.

©DIAGRAM

The slave trade

Most people associate the African slave trade with West Africa and the transport of slaves across the Atlantic to the Americas. But a substantial trade in slaves also existed on the east coast, centered on the island of Zanzibar.

The East African slave trade probably began in the 1200s as a small-scale operation providing slaves from the interior for sale in the local markets of Kilwa and other ports to Swahili merchants. Some of the slaves worked in the merchants' households, on the land, or in local industries, while others were sold on for export to Somalia, Arabia and elsewhere.

By the 1700s the trade was stimulated by Swahili traders on the coast developing extensive plantations of cloves, coconuts, and sisal, and by French merchants growing sugar in the French-owned Indian Ocean islands of Mauritius, Réunion, and later Madagascar. A steady supply of slaves was required both to provide a workforce for these labor-intensive plantations and to use as bearers to carry ivory, copper, and other goods to the coast. The future slaves were acquired by Swahili traders trekking inland and establishing staging posts at such centres as Ujiji, Tabora, and Dodoma in present-day Tanzania. Local peoples would then bring them slaves they had captured for sale, or in exchange for goods, or as tribute. Caravans of slaves were then brought down to the markets on the coast.

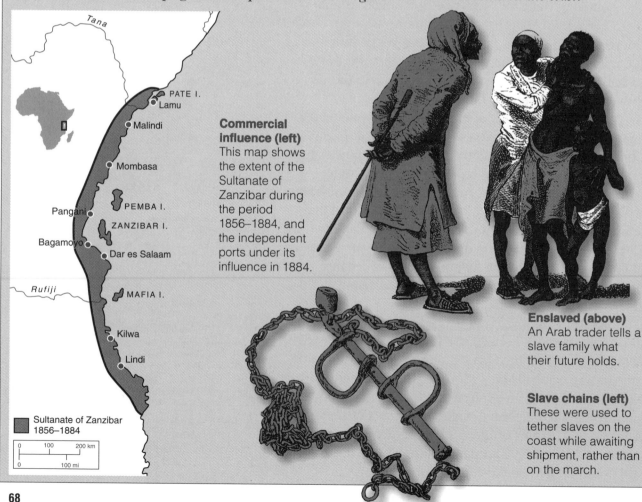

Commercial influence (left)
This map shows the extent of the Sultanate of Zanzibar during the period 1856–1884, and the independent ports under its influence in 1884.

Tana

PATE I.
Lamu
Malindi
Mombasa
Pangani
PEMBA I.
ZANZIBAR I.
Bagamoyo
Dar es Salaam
Rufiji
MAFIA I.
Kilwa
Lindi

Sultanate of Zanzibar
1856–1884

0   100   200 km
0   100 mi

Enslaved (above)
An Arab trader tells a slave family what their future holds.

Slave chains (left)
These were used to tether slaves on the coast while awaiting shipment, rather than on the march.

The wealth of Zanzibar

By the 1860s, 70,000 people a year were being sold as slaves at the Zanzibar slave market alone and many traders made their fortunes in this trade. Mogadishu, Mombasa, Pemba, Zanzibar, and Kilwa all grew rich on this trade.

Nominally the Swahili traders were subjects of the Sultan of Oman, who dominated much of the east coast. In 1840 Sultan Seyyid Said moved the capital of his sultanate from Muscat in the Arabian peninsula to Zanzibar itself, for this was where most of his wealth was now created. By now Zanzibar had become one of the largest trading ports in the Indian Ocean, specializing in ivory and slaves.

After Said's death in 1856, Zanzibar became independent from Oman, but its independence was short-lived. In 1841 the British had appointed a consul to Zanzibar, steadily increasing their influence on the sultan and forcing him to close the slave market in 1873. This influence was resented by Germany, Britain's main rival in the region, which in 1885 took over the sultanate's mainland possessions. Agreement between the two European powers was reached in 1890, allowing Britain to establish a full protectorate over Zanzibar and its island neighbor, Pemba. The independent sultanate was at an end, its territory divided between Germany and Britain.

Humanity on sale!
The Zanzibar slave market in 1872. Although slavery was not new to this region, it reached an unprecedented level in the 19th century. The Zanzibar trade was with Asia and the Middle East, rather than the Americas.

A captured trader
The slave market in Zanzibar was closed by the sultan in 1873. After this time, slave traders were arrested and imprisoned.

© DIAGRAM

The "Scramble" for Africa

In 1880 European contact with East Africa was restricted to trading relations with the main coastal cities, and exploration and some missionary work in the interior. By 1900 the entire region, with the exception of Ethiopia, was in European hands.

In the second half of the 19th century, the unification of first Italy and then Germany created two young and impatient European states anxious to compete for trade and wealth with the established western powers of Britain, France, and to a lesser extent Portugal, and Spain. But while these four powers already had colonial interests in Africa and elsewhere, Italy and Germany had none. Both wanted their place in Africa. This potent combination of economic and political competition, national pride, and imperial pretensions created the "Scramble" for Africa, as it became known.

The scramble was triggered by Leopold II, King of Belgium. Under the guise of the so-called Independent African Association, he made a claim in 1879 for the Congo Basin, which he soon turned into a personal fiefdom. His initiative prompted both France and Britain to follow suit, with France acquiring Tunisia in 1881, and Britain taking Egypt in 1882. Germany responded by seizing land in west and southwest Africa in 1884.

Fearful that land grabs in Africa might cause war in Europe, the German chancellor, Bismarck, convened a conference in Berlin (1884–1885) to regulate the scramble. As a result of this, European states felt free to press their claims without fear of reprisals.

Germany acquired Zanzibar in 1885 and the mainland territories of Tanganyika and Ruanda-Urundi by 1897. Britain established protectorates over the north coast of Somalia in 1884, Uganda in 1888, Zanzibar in 1890, Malawi in 1891, and Kenya in 1895. France acquired a small part of Somalia, at the mouth of the Red Sea, in 1884. Italy consolidated its control of two ports in Eritrea by taking the whole country in 1889, also acquiring the Indian Ocean coast of Somalia in the same year. Its attempt to join its two possessions together by conquering Ethiopia met with failure in 1896.

1885	1889	1892	1908

Germany

German East Africa

These four maps show the extent of control exercised by Germany in East Africa at four critical times in its history: 1885, 1889, 1892 and 1908.

Britain

  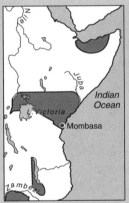 

British East Africa

These four maps show the extent of control exercised by Britain in East Africa at four critical times in its history: 1885, 1889, 1892 and 1908.

Italy

Italian East Africa

These four maps show the extent of control exercised by Italy in East Africa at four critical times in its history: 1885, 1889, 1892 and 1908.

©DIAGRAM

Malawi

Trade with the Arab world and farther east
Exploitation of the indigenous people by Arab slave traders was a source of conflict in East Africa. European involvement in this region was responsible for the reduction in, and eventually led to the abolition of, this barbaric trade in human beings.

The history of Malawi	
1000	Bantu-speaking peoples are established in Malawi
1480	Maravi Confederacy is founded
1600s	Portuguese explore the region but do not settle
1830s	Yao people migrate from Mozambique
1830s	Ngonde people settle in northern Malawi
1859	David Livingstone explores Malawi on his Zambezi expedition
1871	Livingstonia Central Africa Company – later the African Lakes Company – is set up to develop trade links with outside world , thus suppressing slavery
1875	Free Church of Scotland sets up first Christian mission
1889	British agree protection treaties with local rulers
1891	British Central African Protectorate established
1907	Protectorate renamed Nyasaland

The earliest people to inhabit what is now called Malawi – the land to the west and south of Lake Malawi (formerly Nyasa) – were probably hunter-gatherers, but Bantu-speaking immigrants displaced them in the first millennium CE. After 1400 a number of kingdoms developed in the area. Chief among these was the Maravi Confederacy, founded c.1480, which came to dominate the central and southern parts of Malawi.

During the 1830s, Yao people from northern Mozambique migrated into Malawi. One group, the Amchinga, settled at the southeastern corner of Lake Malawi in the 1860s, forming a powerful kingdom led by Makanjila during the next decade. Other Yao leaders established smaller kingdoms or chiefdoms elsewhere in the region. The Yao states became important in the East African trade between the predominantly Swahili coast and the interior, dominating the trade in ivory and slaves around the Lake Malawi region. As a result of this trade, the Yao came under the cultural influence of the Swahili, adopting their Muslim religion, learning Arabic, and wearing Arab clothes.

At about the same time as the Yao arrived in Malawi, the Ngonde people of northern Malawi developed a powerful and wealthy kingdom. The Ngonde lands were situated at an important crossroads of historical trade networks, allowing them to profit from the lucrative ivory trade, but also making them vulnerable to the raids of slave traders. A Swahili slaver set up business in the kingdom, initially with Ngonde consent, but the Swahilis soon attacked Ngonde villages, killing many people.

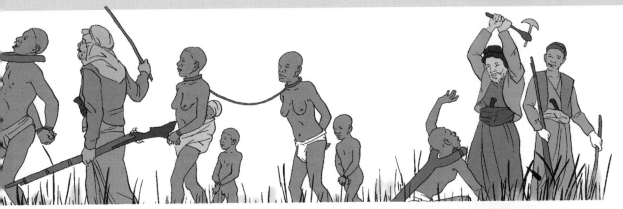

   The slave trade caused wars and great suffering throughout Malawi. Its effects were witnessed by the explorer David Livingstone when he reached the area in 1859. Livingstone introduced Christianity, the Free Church of Scotland sent missionaries to set up missions in 1875, and a trading company was established in 1878 to develop the region. As a result of this involvement in Malawi, Britain made the area a protectorate in 1891, which was originally named the British Central Africa Protectorate but, in 1907, was renamed Nyasaland, a name it kept until independence as Malawi in 1964. Although the British encouraged economic development – constructing roads and railways and introducing cash crops – most of the local people remained poor.

A former British protectorate
This stamp was issued in 1897 when Nyasaland (now known as Malawi) was still part of the British Central Africa Protectorate.

Ivory tusks
Elephants, as well as buffalo and deer, were slaughtered in East Africa for the money their tusks, or horns, would bring when sold overseas. The trade in ivory around the Lake Malawi region was dominated by the Yao states.

© DIAGRAM

Ethiopia in the 19th century

At the start of the 19th century, Ethiopia existed as a country in name only. Muslim Oromo chieftains had set up independent kingdoms across much of the country, notably the powerful kingdom of Begemder in the center and northwest, while the emperor was controlled by Oromo chiefs, who served as ministers and ran the government. The feudal nobility increasingly ran its own lands as independent fiefdoms. Externally, the country was also threatened by Egypt, which under the aggressive leadership of Mehmet Ali had occupied Sudan and was expanding southeast into Ethiopian territory.

The situation changed in the 1850s. In 1853 Kassa, a Christian who led a partisan army against the Egyptians, overthrew the king of Begemder and married the successor to the throne. In 1855 he made himself emperor of Ethiopia, with the title Tewodros (Theodore) II. He removed Oromo control over the central Shoa province in 1856, and consolidated his own power by stripping the nobility of many of their rights. Ethiopia was, however, becoming the subject of much competition among European powers wishing to gain influence in the Horn of Africa. A misunderstanding between Ethiopia and the British led them to send a punitive expedition into Ethiopia in 1868. Tewodros chose to commit suicide rather than surrender to the British troops.

Yohannes IV converted many of his Oromo Muslim subjects to Christianity, reconquered the southern Oromo provinces that had escaped imperial control after the 16th century, and secured the northern border by defeating an Egyptian army in 1877. However, during the 1880s the Mahdist revolt in Sudan threatened his country. Although he defeated the Sudanese in 1889, he died in the battle.

Yohannes IV
A successor to Tewodros II, Yohannes became king of Ethiopia in 1872 and reigned until 1889. Like Tewodros, his policies aimed to maintain the independence of his country from foreign control.

Menelik II

In 1864 Tewodros had appointed Menelik as the governor of the recaptured Shoa province. Menelik succeeded Tewodros as emperor in 1889, taking the title Menelik II, and began an aggressive campaign to rid Ethiopia of its foreign rulers. By 1900 he had expanded his empire deep into the Ogaden region of Somalia and south to the edge of Lake Turkana, giving Ethiopia much the same borders as those it has today.

The greatest threat he faced, however, was from Italy which had no empire but aspired to create a second Roman Empire in the Mediterranean and Red Seas. In 1865 the Italians had established a trading post at the Red Sea port of Aseb in Eritrea, which was formally ceded to them in 1883. They seized Massawa in 1885, and pushed inland until defeated by an Ethiopian army in 1887.

In 1889 Menelik signed the Treaty of Uccialli with the Italians, which gave them partial control over Eritrea. However, Menelik claimed that the Italian version of the treaty declared Ethiopia as its protectorate, to which he would never agree. He therefore renounced the treaty and sent a letter to Italy, France, and Britain – the three European powers interested in Ethiopia – asserting the historic borders of his empire. In response the Italians invaded Tigre province in the north but were decisively defeated at the Battle of Adowa in 1896.

The three powers then signed new treaties with Ethiopia respecting its independence, allowing Ethiopia to remain the only African nation other than Liberia to retain its independence from European control.

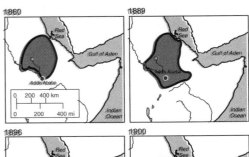

The Empire of Ethiopia
These four maps show the extent of the empire, together with European colonial powers' neighboring possessions from 1860–1900.

The victors at Adowa
Under the command of King Menelik II, Ethiopian forces convincingly defeated the Italian army at the Battle of Adowa in 1896, thus preserving the independence of their country.

© DIAGRAM

East African Asians

There has been an Asian presence on the East African coast for hundreds of years, ever since the first dhows *(cargo-carrying sailboats)* plied the Indian Ocean between India, the Arabian peninsula, and East Africa laden with Indian-made textiles and iron goods in exchange for ivory, gold, and slaves. The sheltered harbors and island anchorages made the coast attractive to Arabic and Indian traders, as did the wealth and variety of goods offered by the various African coastal kingdoms and city-states.

"The Lunatic Line"

The majority of the present-day Asian community, however, owes its presence in East Africa to the construction by the British of the East Africa Railway (1896–1902), linking the port of Mombasa with Lake Victoria. The line was designed to enable British troops to move quickly inland to put down any local disturbances or revolts in Britain's newly won East African empire. Many of these workers died of tropical diseases, while others returned to India on completion of their contracts. "The Lunatic Line," as it was dubbed by its critics, was built across hazardous and difficult terrain, including deserts, the Great Rift Valley, and tsetse-fly-infested land.

After the railway was built, 7,000 Indians chose to settle in the region, bringing their families with them while still retaining close links with India. Although some Indians continued to work on the railways, most established themselves as merchants, initially catering to the needs of fellow Indians, but soon expanding to sell to the native African population. Hearing of the business opportunities in the region, Indian immigrants continued to arrive in Africa in the 1920s, by which time Asians, through

their trading activities, had done much to integrate areas of the region into the cash economy.

Uneasy settlers

The East African National Congress was formed in 1914 to represent the interests of the Asian community, particularly in demanding equal representation with Europeans on the legislative councils, equal economic opportunities (especially in relation to land ownership in the Kenyan highlands), and in opposing segregation between Europeans and Asians. Their complaints were principally aimed at the community of European settlers, whom they far outnumbered. In marked contrast to the Indian community in South Africa, and despite the urging of political leaders in India itself, East African Asians rarely took up common cause with the African population toward whom they tended to feel culturally superior.

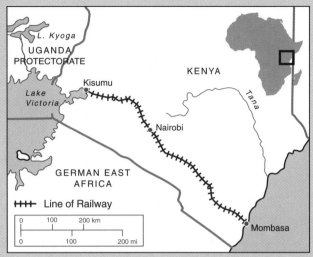

"The Lunatic Line," or East Africa Railway
This was constructed for economic and strategic reasons by the British when they declared Kenya a protectorate in 1895. The first line was laid at Mombasa in 1896, reached Nairobi in 1899, and Kisumu in 1901.

Constructing the railway
As local African labor proved to be either unavailable, unreliable, or hostile, 32,000 workers were recruited in the then British-run India. Over 2,500 laborers tragically lost their lives, and a further 6,000 were seriously injured during the construction of the railway.

After the "Scramble"

Survivor
This field gun was typical of those used by the German Army in East Africa during its campaign in World War I.

An *askari*
During World War I many black Africans fought in the colonial armies of German East Africa. This Swahili sculpture portrays one of these soldiers, known as *askari*, after the Swahili word for a soldier.

After the "Scramble" for Africa ended in the mid-1890s, a number of border changes altered the political map of East Africa in the next two decades, chiefly delineating Ethiopia's borders with British and Italian Somaliland and with Kenya, and the border between Uganda and Kenya. What were once protectorates, such as Italian Somaliland, became colonies as the European powers consolidated their control over the region.

World War I

The main change occurred after 1914. The outbreak of war in August 1914 pitted Germany on the one side against Britain and France on the other, joined by Italy in May 1915. While the main fighting was in Europe, war broke out in East Africa as British troops from Kenya and Belgian troops from the Congo attempted to conquer German East Africa. Other German colonies in Africa – Togo, Cameroon, and Southwest Africa (now Namibia) – were quickly overrun by Allied troops, but the German commander in East Africa, General Paul von Lettow-Vorbeck, proved a formidable adversary.

At the start of the war von Lettow-Vorbeck inflicted two defeats on British troops but, by 1916, the British had the upper hand as more Allied troops became available following the surrender of German troops elsewhere on the continent. The general then abandoned conventional warfare and took up guerrilla-style conflict, using superior mobility and acclimatized African troops to evade capture. In November 1917, as the Allied armies closed in, he slipped across the border into supposedly

neutral Portuguese Mozambique, reentering Tanganyika in January 1918. He then marched along the north of Lake Malawi and quickly invaded British-owned Northern Rhodesia (now Zambia). For the rest of the year, he and his army eluded capture, only surrendering on November 25, 1918 after he heard that an armistice had been signed in Europe two weeks earlier; he was the last German commander to surrender.

Post-war East Africa

As a result of the peace settlements of 1919, German East Africa was divided between Britain and Belgium, with Britain acquiring Tanganyika and Belgium controlling Ruanda-Urundi. Both of these were technically not colonies but mandates of the League of Nations, a new international organization set up to ensure world peace and ultimately responsible for the government of these and other mandated territories in Africa, the Middle East, and the Pacific.

However, while the three victorious colonial powers of East Africa – Britain, France, and Italy – were all founder members of the League, none of their colonial possessions in the region were eligible to join. Only Ethiopia, often known in this period as Abyssinia, became a member in 1923.

Two years later, Britain and Italy reached agreement about the border between Italian Somaliland and Kenya, with Britain ceding a strip of land known as Jubaland to the Italians. The post-war map of East Africa was now firmly in place for the foreseeable future.

Embarking for the front, Nairobi
War broke out in East Africa as British and Belgian troops attempted to conquer German East Africa.

General Paul von Lettow-Vorbeck
He commanded the German troops in East Africa at the start of World War I. A formidable adversary, he only surrendered to the British after an armistice had been signed in Europe.

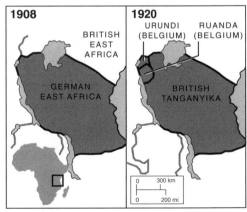

The origin of Tanganyika
In the late 1800s, a number of European states were interested in the area that became known as Tanganyika. The map (left) shows the extent of colonial control in 1908 and the map (right) that in 1920.

© DIAGRAM

Mutesa, king of Buganda
Traditional rulers, including the Mutesas of Buganda, opposed British attempts to impose their rule in areas of East Africa.

Although the imposition of European rule across almost the whole of East Africa – from the British and French takeover of northern Somalia in 1884 to the establishment of the British protectorate over Kenya in 1895 – was extraordinarily quick, it was not accepted without opposition. Across the region, peoples fought against the European colonists, most notably the Ethiopians against the Italians at Dogali in 1887 and then decisively at the Battle of Adowa in 1896.

Other nations and peoples were not successful in preventing a takeover of their lands, but both the German and British colonizers were met with stiff resistance in their East African protectorates and colonies.

In German-occupied Tanganyika, the coastal Swahilis and the mainland Hehe, Mbunga, Pogoro, and Nyamwezi all fought tenaciously between 1888 and 1902, while the Germans were forced to put down the lengthy Maji Maji rising in the south of the country between 1905 and 1907 with great force.

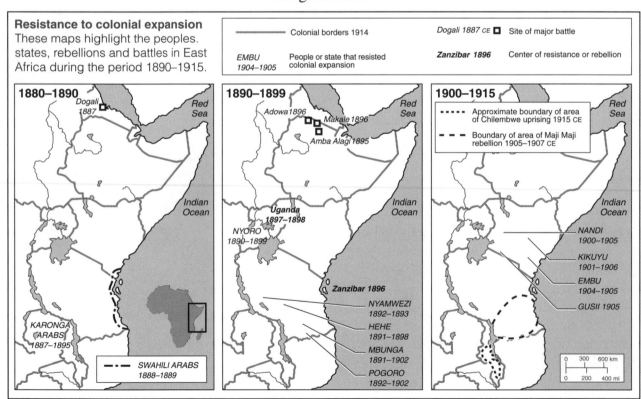

Resistance to colonial expansion
These maps highlight the peoples, states, rebellions and battles in East Africa during the period 1890–1915.

———— Colonial borders 1914

EMBU 1904–1905 People or state that resisted colonial expansion

Dogali 1887 CE ☐ Site of major battle

Zanzibar 1896 Center of resistance or rebellion

1880–1890
Dogali 1887
Red Sea
Indian Ocean
KARONGA ARABS 1887–1895
— ·· — SWAHILI ARABS 1888–1889

1890–1899
Adowa 1896
Makale 1896
Amba Alagi 1895
Red Sea
Uganda 1897–1898
NYORO 1890–1899
Indian Ocean
Zanzibar 1896
NYAMWEZI 1892–1893
HEHE 1891–1898
MBUNGA 1891–1902
POGORO 1892–1902

1900–1915
····· Approximate boundary of area of Chilembwe uprising 1915 CE
— — — Boundary of area of Maji Maji rebellion 1905–1907 CE
Red Sea
Indian Ocean
NANDI 1900–1905
KIKUYU 1901–1906
EMBU 1904–1905
GUSII 1905
0 300 600 km
0 200 400 mi

The British also encountered opposition to their rule. In Uganda, the Nyoro put up spirited resistance between 1890 and 1899; in 1897–1898 the traditional rulers of Uganda, including the Mutesas of Buganda, led a more serious uprising. Zanzibar rose in revolt in 1896 while, in Kenya, the British met opposition from the Nandi, Kikuyu, Embu, and Gusii between 1900 and 1906. In both British and Italian Somaliland, Sayyid Muhammad, rudely called the "Mad Mullah," put up prolonged resistance to colonial rule between 1891 and 1920.

The Chilembwe Revolt

One of the most significant uprisings against colonial rule took place in Malawi, which had become a British Protectorate in 1891. The Karonga Arabs had already resisted the British in the north of the country between 1887 and 1895, but a more serious revolt broke out in 1915 in the south of the country. It was led by the Reverend John Chilembwe (c.1860–1915), a Baptist minister who had studied theology in the US and founded the Providence Industrial Mission at Mbombwe in 1900, which later set up seven schools elsewhere in the country. In 1915, provoked by the cruelty of the white plantation owners, Chilembwe led a revolt against British rule. It failed and he was captured and shot.

Resistance to colonial rule	
1887	Ethiopians defeat Italian at Dogali
1887–1895	Karonga Arabs resist British in Malawi
1888–1889	Swahilis revolt against Germans in coastal Tanganyika
1890–1899	Nyoro resist British in Uganda
1891–1898	Hehe revolt against Germans in Tanganyika
1891–1920	Sayyid Muhammad leads resistance to British and Italian rule in Somalia
1892	Nyamwezi (to 1893) and Pogoro (to 1902) revolt against Germans in Tanganyika
1895	Ethiopians defeat Italians at Amba Alagi
1896	Ethiopians defeat Italians at Makale and again, decisively, at Adowa
1896	Zanzibar revolts against British rule
1897–1898	Widespread resistance in Uganda to British rule
1900–1905	Nandi resist British in Kenya
1901–1906	Kikuyu resist British in Kenya
1904–1905	Embu and Gusii resist British in Kenya
1905–1907	Maji Maji revolt against Germans in Tanganyika
1915	Rev. John Chilembwe leads revolt in Malawi against British colonial rule

Execution (left)
German soldiers are shown here hanging Africans durring the Maji Maji rising in East Africa in 1905.

Rebellion (right)
Intertribal solidarity confronted German rule in East Africa in what became known as the Maji Maji rising, 1905.

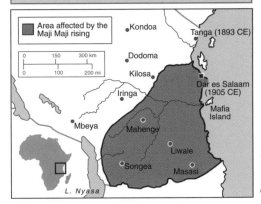

© DIAGRAM

The Battle of Adowa, 1896
This battle, in which Ethiopian forces defeated the Italians, was commemorated in many forms, one of which was this drawing, presently housed in Addis Ababa University.

After the decisive defeat of the Italians at Adowa in 1896, Emperor Menelik II moved quickly to secure his state. He doubled his empire's size to within its old historical limits by 1900, pushing east into the remains of the Oromo lands and the Ogaden region and southwest towards Lake Turkana. In 1896–1897 he signed treaties with the three colonial powers with interests in the region – Britain, France, and Italy – defining Ethiopia's borders and protecting its independence. In addition, Italy agreed to pay compensation for its invasion.

Menelik's rule over his empire was a mixture of the progressive and the reactionary. He expanded the capital, Addis Ababa, built railways and roads, attempted to end the slave trade, and curbed the feudal nobility. However, he turned the defeated Oromo into slaves – he and his wife Queen Taitu personally owned 70,000 of them – and allowed little democracy in his country.

The final years of his reign were marked by illness and decline. In 1902 the British forced him to sign a treaty forbidding his free use of the annual floods of the Blue Nile, while a tripartite treaty in 1906 between Britain, France, and Italy gave them new rights to Ethiopia, a treaty Menelik could not resist. In 1908 he was forced to accept a treaty with Italy for the delimitation of the Somali border, which later gave Italy a pretext for launching its invasion into Ogaden in 1935.

The regency

In 1913 Menelik died, aged 69. His heir *Ras* Makonnen had died in 1906, leaving the succession in the hands of Menelik's grandson, Lij Iyasu. A regency was set up to prepare him for his role, as he was still a minor, but Iyasu refused to accept its tutelage. When he ascended to the throne, aged 17, he proved incapable of governing. He allied himself with Sayyid Muhammad in his revolt against the British and Italians in Somalia, sided with the Germans and Turks in World War I at a time when both were trying to gain control of his country, and converted to Islam. In 1916 the church and nobility led a revolt against him. In his place, Menelik's daughter Zauditu (Zawditu) became empress assisted by a regent, *Ras* Tafari, son of *Ras* Makonnen, as her heir apparent.

The change of emperor was just in time, for the 1915 Treaty of London had promised Ethiopia to Italy if it entered World War I on the British side. Tafari reversed his predecessor's policies and supported Britain and Italy. As a member of the League of Nations, Ethiopia was able to takes its place on the world stage. Zauditu protested strongly against a new British plan for dividing up Ethiopia into spheres of foreign influence in 1926, and obtained access to the Red Sea through the Italian port of Aseb in Eritrea in 1928.

In 1930 Zauditu died and Tafari became emperor, adopting the name of Haile Selassie. He introduced a new constitution, limited parliamentary democracy, and also began a large program of modernization.

Menelik II
He was the king of Shoa, the central province of Ethiopia. In 1896 he convincingly defeated an Italian army at the Battle of Adowa, thus preserving Ethiopia's independence.

Haile Selassie I
Originally called *Ras* (Prince) Tafari, he was Emperor of Ethiopia from 1930 until he was deposed by the army in 1974. He became revered as a divine being by the Rastafarian religious group, which is named after him.

©DIAGRAM

Ethiopia at war

Resisting the onslaught
With the help of only outmoded weapons, Ethiopians tried unsuccessfully to halt the invasion of Italian forces in 1936.

Ethiopia: towards independence

1896	Ethiopians defeat Italians at Adowa
1896–	Menelik II signs treaties with
1897	colonial powers defining his borders
1902	Anglo-Ethiopian Treaty prevents Ethiopians using the waters of the Blue Nile, and defines border with Anglo–Egyptian Sudan
1906	Tripartite Treaty limits Ethiopian independence
1907	Border with British Kenya defined
1908	Border with Italian Somaliland defined
1913	Death of Menelik II
1916	Emperor Lij Iyasu deposed; Zauditu becomes empress with *Ras* Tafari as regent and heir apparent
1923	Ethiopia joins League of Nations
1930	Zauditu dies; *Ras* Tafari becomes emperor as Haile Selassie
1931	Ethiopia acquires a written constitution
1935	Italian invasion of Ethiopia
1936	Haile Selassie goes into exile
1941	British army expels Italians from East Africa; Haile Selassie resumes his throne
1952	Eritrea federated with Ethiopia
1962	Eritrea is absorbed into Ethiopia

Haile Selassie's empire was still threatened by Italy, despite its defeat in 1896. In 1928–1930 the government of the Italian dictator Mussolini began to remove from its maps the defined frontier between Ethiopia and its two East African colonies – Eritrea and Somalia – and press its claim for border readjustments, despite the 1897 and 1908 treaties it had signed with Ethiopia. Mussolini launched a major international propaganda war against Ethiopia and sent an expeditionary force into the country from Italian Somaliland. On December 5, 1934 the two sides clashed at the oasis at Walwal, 50 miles into Ethiopia; 100 Ethiopians were killed.

Both sides then took their dispute to the League of Nations, but discussions between December 1934 and March 1935 reached an impasse. On October 2, 1935 Italy invaded Ethiopia without any declaration of war.

Although the League of Nations condemned the action and imposed limited sanctions, Italy gained a huge international advantage by the pact agreed in December between Sir Samuel Hoare and Pierre Laval, respectively British foreign secretary and French prime minister, by which the two powers agreed to the partition of Ethiopia with Italy in an attempt to appease Mussolini, and also to prevent him allying with Nazi Germany. The failure of the sanctions, its inability to deter aggression, and the existence of a pact between two of its leading supporters which went against its own principles, seriously undermined the League of Nations as an international organization at a time when Italy, Germany, and Japan were all engaged in aggressive expansion.

The Ethiopians were soon overwhelmed by the modern tanks, aircraft, and equipment of the Italians – who used poison gas against army and civilians alike – and were decisively defeated near Maiceu in northern Tigre in early April 1936. On May 5, the Italian army entered Addis Ababa, and Haile Selassie went into exile, pleading his nation's case in person at the League on June 30. The Italians soon enforced control, executing Archbishop Petros, head of the Coptic church, massacring monks, and putting down a three-day rising in Addis Ababa in February 1937 with considerable ferocity. Sporadic resistance by the Black Lions guerrilla movement continued, however, and Italy never totally subdued the country.

A new empire!
This Italian poster shows a Blackshirt (Italian Fascist) attempting to carve out a Roman Empire for the 20th century in Ethiopia.

Liberation

On June 10, 1940, Italy declared war on Britain and France and invaded Kenya and British Somaliland, occupying the latter in August, and incorporating it into an Italian empire that occupied the whole of the Horn of Africa apart from the small French Somali enclave.

This empire was to be short-lived, however, for in January 1941 British and Commonwealth troops invaded Eritrea from Sudan and Somaliland from Kenya. By April 1941 they had linked up with the Ethiopian resistance to liberate Addis Ababa, and also to end Italian control over the region.

Haile Selassie returned to his country on May 5, 1941, resuming full control of his country from the British in January 1942, although Ogaden remained under British military control until 1948. In the post-war settlement, Italian Eritrea remained under British control until September 1952 when, after a United Nations sponsored referendum, it was federated with Ethiopia, becoming an integral part of the empire in 1962.

An advocate for peace
Once economic sanctions against a hostile Italy proved to be ineffectual, Emperor Haile Selassie was forced to plead the case for his nation at the League of Nations in 1936.

© DIAGRAM

The Mau Mau rebellion in Kenya

Jomo Kenyatta
He was the first prime minister of a newly-independent Kenya in 1963. During his presidency (1964–1978) he encouraged ethnic and racial harmony, and presided over a thriving economy and an expansion of tourism.

The Kikuyu people of Kenya — the country's largest ethnic group — live in Kikuyuland on the highland plateau at the foot of Mount Kenya. An agricultural people, they traded their produce in return for hides and livestock with their neighbors, the Maasai, with whom they were on good terms.

This settled existence was radically disturbed by the European "scramble" for African colonies. In 1895 the British made Kenya a protectorate. They built the capital city of Nairobi in the south of Kikuyuland, and constructed the East Africa Railway from the coast up through Kikuyuland to Lake Victoria. European settlers also took over land from the Kikuyu in what became known as the White Highlands, confining the Kikuyu to a small reserve where it was difficult to farm. Many Kikuyu were forced to leave the land and work for the settlers, or in factories that sprang up in Nairobi. British officials ruled the colony and the Kikuyu became third-class citizens in their own country (the Asian workers on the railroad were the second class). Many Kikuyu men worked as carriers for British troops during World War I.

The rebellion

In 1920 the Kikuyu Central Association was established, partly in response to the discrimination experienced by Kikuyu veterans. Many Kikuyu men took up arms again in World War II, fighting against the Germans, and again after the war they were bitter about their treatment. As a result of these experiences, the Kikuyu joined with others to organize opposition to the colonial power, forming the Kenya African Union (KAU) in 1944. Post-war white immigration to Kenya exacerbated the situation. When progress towards independence seemed slow, some Kikuyu nationalists organized a secret

After the end of the uprising, a new generation of politicians, led by Tom Mboya, continued the struggle for independence. In 1961 elections were held for a new parliament. The Kikuyu-dominated Kenya African National Union (KANU) won a majority, but refused to take office until Kenyatta was released. The main opposition party, the Kenya African Democratic Union (KADU) then formed a government. In August 1961 Kenyatta was freed and a KANU–KADU coalition was formed.

Kenya became independent on December 12, 1963, with Kenyatta as its first prime minister. In 1964 Kenya became a republic with Kenyatta as president. KANU and KADU merged, in effect making Kenya a one-party state.

Detention camp, Nyeri, Kenya
This was set up by the British in the 1950s to hold those suspected of involvement in the Mau Mau rebellion.

society, called the Mau Mau, inside the KAU which in fall 1952 started to commit acts of terrorism against white settlers and African – often fellow Kikuyu – supporters of British rule.

Fighting between the Kikuyu and British troops continued until 1956, during which time 11,000 Africans, mostly Kikuyu, were killed; up to 10,000 British troops were involved in suppressing the uprising. More than 50,000 people were imprisoned in detention camps, notably Jomo Kenyatta who, as the senior nationalist politician in the country, was imprisoned in 1953. He was convicted of leading the Mau Mau movement, a charge he denied.

In many ways, the Mau Mau rebellion was a generational conflict, with young men who had served in the British army during the war, and so gained a wider experience of the world, fighting against their more cautious elders who accepted continuing British rule.

For their part, the British had no wish to see a white settler state established in Kenya, and were prompted by the uprising to introduce some much-needed social and political reforms.

Camps and conflicts (above)
This map shows the location of the detention camps, and the principal areas of conflict, during the Mau Mau rebellion in the 1950s in Kenya.

Camp prisoners (left)
Alleged supporters of the Mau Mau rebellion were kept in detention camps during the conflict.

© DIAGRAM

87

From colonies to independent nations

At the end of World War II, the only independent nation in East Africa was Ethiopia. The rest were still colonies of the French, British, and Belgian empires. Within about 30 years, however, the European colonial era was at an end, and all the countries were independent.

The European colonial era had a profound impact on the region. It set the modern international boundaries and molded the national economies into their present dependence on the export of raw materials rather than manufactured goods. However, the handover from European to African rule was in the main peaceful, in contrast to the violence that preceded or accompanied it elsewhere in the continent, notably in Algeria, the Belgian Congo, and the former Portuguese colonies, such as Angola and Mozambique. The national movements that arose largely collaborated with their colonial rulers to achieve independence.

British East Africa

The British first granted some internal self-government in their colonies before handing over complete control upon independence. In Tanganyika, Julius Nyerere and others founded the Tanganyika African National Union (TANU) in 1954 to press for independence. Britain granted the country internal self-government in 1958, and full independence in December 1961. Zanzibar gained its own independence from Britain in December 1963 and, following the overthrow of the sultan and the declaration of a republic in January 1964, merged with Tanganyika to form Tanzania in April 1964. Kenya followed a similar path once the Mau Mau rebellion was crushed, with self-government in 1961 followed by independence in December 1963.

In Uganda, the British had divided the country into five regions, four of which were under direct British administration with the help of local chiefs, while the fifth, Buganda, was ruled by its prince, the *Kabaka*, under the British crown. A ministerial system of government was set up in 1955 and the country became fully independent in 1962. A year later, Uganda became a republic, with the ruling *Kabaka* as the first president.

The situation in Nyasaland was more complex, as in 1953 the British linked it with Northern and Southern Rhodesia in the Central African Federation. The Malawi National Congress, led by Dr Hastings Banda, resisted white Rhodesian domination of their country, which was allowed to secede in 1963, when it gained internal self-government. Full independence happened in July 1964.

Somalia

Following the defeat of the Italians in 1941, Britain assumed control over Italian Somaliland. In 1950 the United Nations gave Italy trusteeship over its former colony, which in 1960 merged with British Somaliland as the independent republic of Somalia. Eritrea became a part of Ethiopia.

In French Somaliland, the majority Somali Issa people and others began to press for independence in the 1940s. However, in 1958, the majority voted to make the colony an autonomous state in the French Union. In 1967 a second referendum was held, in which 60 percent voted to remain French; the country was renamed the French Territory of the Afars and Issas. During the 1970s the influence of the Issa grew, largely due to immigration from Somalia and because the new French citizenship law discriminated against them. A third referendum was held, resulting in a huge vote in favour of independence, and the Republic of Djibouti was created in June 1977.

Ruanda-Urundi

The exception to this peaceful transition to independence occurred in the Belgian mandated territory of Ruanda-Urundi. Governed as part of the Belgian Congo from 1922, the two were separated when the Congo became independent in June 1960. By this time, an outbreak of communal violence between Hutus and Tutsis had caused thousands of deaths. In 1961 a referendum was held in which Urundi voted to become an independent monarchy under the Tutsi Mwambutsa IV, who had ruled since 1915, while Ruanda voted to become a republic. The territory was then split into Burundi and Rwanda, both countries becoming independent in July 1962.

Independence
Stamps were issued to mark the newly won state of independence of the following African nations: Kenya (1963); Malawi (1964); Uganda (1962); and Tanganyika (1961).

The Seychelles

Arab traders may have visited the Seychelles in the first millennium CE, but Portuguese mariners are credited with the first recorded sighting in 1505. A century later, in 1609, an expedition launched by the English East India Company made the first known landing, reporting that the islands were uninhabited. In the early 18th century, pirates used the islands as a source of water, food, and shelter.

In 1742 the French rulers of the Ile de France (now Mauritius) sent an exploratory expedition, but they did not annex the islands until 1756 in an attempt to prevent an English occupation. The French named the islands the Séchelles, which the British later changed to Seychelles.

The first French colonists arrived in 1770 to create a supply station for French ships sailing to southern Asia. However, they also cut down the forests and killed wildlife, including giant tortoises, greatly damaging the environment. Such destruction was curtailed in the early 1790s.

British islands

In 1794 – as Britain and France fought in the wars of the French Revolution – Britain demanded the surrender of the islands, which were officially ceded in 1815. The British made the islands a dependency of Mauritius, also taken from France.

After 1833 and the abolition of slavery in the British Empire, the settlers cultivated crops such as coconuts, cinnamon, and vanilla, which were less labor-intensive than crops grown earlier. Britain made the Seychelles a separate colony in 1903, and set up the first legislative council in 1948.

In 1964 two political parties were formed: the right-wing Seychelles Democratic Party (SDP) of James Mancham, which opposed independence in favor of some kind of association with Britain, and the left-wing Seychelles People's United Party (SPUP) of France-Albert René, which favored independence. The SDP won a majority in the 1970 election and Mancham became prime minister. It increased its majority in 1974, when it adopted pro-independence policies after a strong swing in public opinion against continuing British rule.

The Seychelles achieved internal self-government on October 1, 1975, and full independence as a republic in the Commonwealth on June 29, 1976.

Supply station (left)
The Seychelles were explored in 1742 by France, and later annexed in 1756, However, the first French colonists did not arrive until 1770, accompanied by African slaves, to create a supply station for merchant ships en route to trade with countries in southern Asia.

After independence

As president, James Mancham appointed René as his prime minister but, after disagreements developed between the two, Mancham was deposed in a bloodless coup in 1977, and René became president.

René suspended the constitution, dissolved the national assembly, and introduced socialist policies. In 1979, fearing that he too might be deposed, René made his Seychelles People's Progressive Front (SPPF) the sole legal party.

As president, René survived an attempt by South African mercenaries to restore Mancham to power in 1980, an army mutiny in 1982, and several other coups. The only candidate in the 1979, 1984, and 1991 presidential elections, René eventually legalized opposition parties after pressure from foreign aid donors. Although Mancham stood against him, René was reelected in 1993 and again in 1998 and 2001. Under René, the country's economy has developed quickly, with tourism as the leading source of income.

King Prempe
The last great king of the Asante in what is now Ghana, he became king in 1888, and resisted British attempts to colonize his kingdom. He was deposed, and spent some time in exile in the Seychelles c.1908.

Kabarega
He was the leader of the historic kingdom of Bunyoro which, with Buganda, formed the basis of the modern state of Uganda. Like King Prempe of the Asante, he was also exiled in the Seychelles.

A double celebration (right)
A stamp issued in 1976 marking the independence of Seychelles and also the US Bicentenary.

SEYCHELLES R1
UNITED STATES INDEPENDENCE 1776
SEYCHELLES INDEPENDENCE 1976

© DIAGRAM

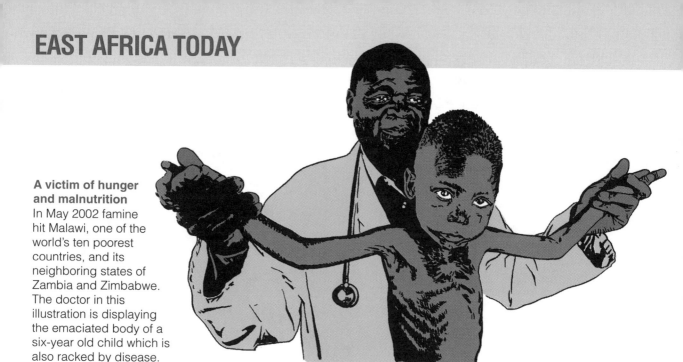

A victim of hunger and malnutrition
In May 2002 famine hit Malawi, one of the world's ten poorest countries, and its neighboring states of Zambia and Zimbabwe. The doctor in this illustration is displaying the emaciated body of a six-year old child which is also racked by disease.

World AIDS Day, 1991
This Ethiopian stamp graphically demonstrates the seriousness, and the horror, of the crisis facing the world owing to the spread of AIDS for which, more than ten years later, there was still no known cure.

Despite its abundant human and environmental resources, East Africa is the poorest of the five regions of the continent. It lacks the mineral and fossil fuel reserves of other areas, and its economic development has been hampered by political and ethnic turmoil. About 85 percent of the people make their living as subsistence farmers, contributing little to the national economy. Droughts, famines, and more recently floods, have also caused great suffering and hardship.

Judged by their per capita gross national product (GNP) in 1999, Ethiopia, Burundi, and Malawi are the poorest countries, although Somalia would join that list at the bottom if reliable figures were available for comparison, for the country has in effect collapsed and is divided into three territories. Civil war and other conflicts have affected the economic development of Eritrea and Ethiopia, while both Burundi and Rwanda have been affected by appalling conflict between Hutu and Tutsi and, in the case of Rwanda, genocide. Uganda has only recently begun to recover after decades of political and military mismanagement.

Only the Seychelles, with a per capita income in 2000 of US $7,050, has advanced economically in recent years, largely due to its earnings from tourism.

Per Capita Gross National Income in US$

$ = $1,000

Seychelles	Djibouti	Kenya	Uganda	Tanzania	Rwanda	Malawi	Eritrea	Burundi	Ethiopia	Somalia	US
7,310	890	350	310	280	220	170	170	110	110	?	34,100

Political instability

Politically, East Africa has suffered from military coups, revolutions, dictatorships, and long periods of one-party government. Many of the countries gaining independence in the 1960s rapidly changed their constitutions to become republics and then established one-party states. Most of these have been dismantled and multiparty democracy is now encouraged.

Tanzania, which in the years after independence, pursued a policy of "African socialism" based on *ujc* a Swahili term meaning familyhood and self-reliance has now adopted a multiparty system and more liber. economic policies closer in style to the free enterprise approach of Kenya. But while Kenya became the most stable of East African nations and one of the richest, it remained strongly autocratic in government. The revival in 1999 of the East African Community by Kenya, Tanzania, and Uganda with the aim of establishing a customs union, a common market, a monetary union, and ultimately a political union, might bring greater prosperity to the three countries.

East African income compared with the US
This diagram shows the per capita estimated gross national income (GNI), previously known as the gross national product (GNP), of the East African states in 2000. GNI is the official measure of the size of the individual economies in the region.

Handling cotton
Although cotton had been found growing wild in Uganda, it was not until 1904 that imported cotton seed was introduced. By 1914, cotton had become the major export.

©DIAGRAM

93

Uganda since independence

Milton Obote
He became the first prime minister of a newly independent Uganda in 1962, but was deposed by Idi Amin in 1971. He returned as president in 1980, but was deposed again in 1985.

Yoweri Museveni
He took part in the overthrow of Idi Amin in 1979, and became president of Uganda in 1986 following a five-year conflict with forces of the government.

Idi Amin
In 1971 he seized power in Uganda. Initially a popular leader, he went on to create a repressive regime under which many thousands were exiled or, even worse, executed.

Of all the countries which comprise East Africa, Uganda has had one of the most troubled histories. The country became independent from Britain in 1962 with Milton Obote as its first prime minister. The next year, Uganda became a republic, with the ruling *Kabaka* of Buganda as its first president, but disputes with Obote led to his dismissal in 1966.

Under a new constitution adopted in 1967, Obote himself became president and the traditional kingdoms were abolished (they were restored in 1992, but with limited powers only).

In 1971 Major General Idi Amin seized power in a army coup and became president. Amin soon launched a reign of terror against his opponents and thousands were murdered. In 1978 Ugandan troops invaded Tanzania in a border dispute. In response, Ugandan rebels led by Yoweri Museveni and aided by the Tanzanian army invaded the country in 1979 and overthrew Amin, who fled into exile.

Obote was reelected president in 1980, but following charges of electoral fraud, the National Resistance Movement (NRM) led by Museveni launched a civil war. After five years of increasingly repressive rule, Obote was removed in a military coup. The NRM seized power the following year, with Museveni becoming president.

Female recruits
Many women joined the Tanzanian People's Militia, which helped in the invasion of Uganda.

Non-party government

Following these years of instability, often fuelled by racial and tribal tension, Museveni instituted a non-party system of government as the best way to achieve stability, a system endorsed in a referendum in 2000. Museveni was reelected president in both 1996 and 2001, introducing economic and social reforms that have made Uganda one of the success stories of modern-day Africa. The revival of the East African Community with Kenya and Tanzania in 1999 – it had collapsed in 1977 as a result of Amin's hostile policy to the two other members – holds out hope of stronger economic growth.

Museveni had to face a number of problems, not least the growing spread of AIDS, which the government attacked with an education campaign that reduced the infection rate from 14 percent in the early 1990s to 8 percent and falling by 2002. In the north of the country, the Lord's Resistance Army has conducted guerrilla campaigns against the government throughout the 1990s while, from 1998–2002, Uganda was involved in the civil war in the neighboring Democratic Republic of the Congo.

East Africa's Asians

The Asian community was one of those most affected by Uganda's instability. At independence, as elsewhere in East Africa, Asians were given a choice of becoming citizens of their new countries, or retaining British nationality but without the right of residency in Britain. Most felt that their security in Africa was limited and thus kept their British nationality. In Kenya, Africanization policies led to a gradual loss of jobs and status, but the change was handled with minimal disruption.

In Uganda, however, the change was sudden and brutal. In 1972 Idi Amin expelled the entire Asian community of 80,000 people, redistributing their businesses to government supporters. Although the expulsions were popular in Uganda, they had a devastating effect on the economy from which the country is still recovering. As a result, President Museveni encouraged the exiled Asian community to return home during the 1990s.

Events since independence	
1962	Uganda wins independence from Britain with Milton Obote as prime minister
1963	Uganda becomes a republic
1966	The *Kabaka* of Buganda (president), is removed by Obote
1967	Uganda, Kenya, and Tanzania form East African Community
1967	Obote introduces new constitution with himself as president
1971	Army coup overthrows Obote; Idi Amin becomes president
1972	Asians expelled from Uganda
1977	East African Community collapses
1978	Ugandan troops invade Tanzania following a border dispute
1979	Ugandan rebels and Tanzanian army overthrows Amin
1980	Obote reelected president
1981	Yoweri Museveni founds the National Resistance Movement (NRM) and starts guerrilla war against Obote
1985	Obote removed in a military coup
1986	NRM seizes power; Museveni becomes president
1986–1994	NRM's council serves as Uganda's legislature
1992	Traditional kingdoms restored with limited powers
1995	Museveni institutes a non-party system of government
1996	Museveni reelected
1998	Uganda intervenes in Congo civil war
1999	East African Community reactivated
1999	Uganda and Sudan sign a peace agreement to settle outstanding disputes
2000	Referendum endorses non-party system of government
2001	Museveni reelected

©DIAGRAM

Ethiopia and Eritrea

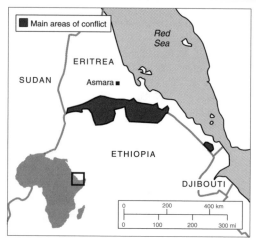

Disputed territory
This map shows the main areas of conflict between Ethiopia and Eritrea during the period 1998–2000.

EPLF insignia
The Eritrean Popular (or People's) LIberation Front (EPLF) launched a movement fighting for independence from Ethiopia in the 1960s. In 1993, the EPLF finally achieved their goal when Eritrea was liberated from Ethiopia.

Conflict in the Ogaden
In 1964 and 1977, Somalia and Ethiopia come into conflict over the Ogaden region of Ethiopia, which is inhabited largely by ethnic Somalis. These Ethiopian conscripts are on parade in Addis Ababa.

On his return to Ethiopia after the defeat of the occupying Italians in 1941, Emperor Haile Selassie continued with his reforms to modernize his country. The former Italian colony of Eritrea was federated with Ethiopia in 1952 and made a full province of the empire in 1962, against the wishes of the Eritrean Liberation Front (ELF), which had started a war for independence in 1961 that would last for another 30 years.

Haile Selassie's reforms were slow, however, and after a prolonged drought and famine from 1972–1974, a military coup overthrew the emperor and declared a socialist republic. Haile-Mariam Mengistu, who became head of state in 1977, had many opponents killed, but broke up the estates of the large landowners.

But the new government faced many problems arising from Ethiopia's ethnic diversity. In addition to the secessionist war in Eritrea, the government also had to contain the Tigre People's Liberation Front and the invasion in 1977 by Somali forces to support the ethnic uprising in the Ogaden, an uprising that continued long after the Somali army was evicted in 1979. A peace treaty between the two countries was eventually signed in 1988.

Independence and war
Eritrean and Tigrean forces finally defeated the Mengistu regime in 1991. The Tigrean-dominated Ethiopian People's Revolutionary Democratic Front set up a transitional government in Addis Ababa headed by Meles

On the brink of death
Not only victims of the prolonged drought in Ethiopia from 1984–1987, these unfortunate children were also displaced from their homelands by a combination of civil wars and hostile invasions from neighboring countries.

Ethiopia and Eritrea in conflict	
1941	Emperor Haile Selassie returns to Ethiopia after defeat of Italians
1952	Eritrea federated with Ethiopia
1961	Eritrean People's Liberation Front (EPLF) begins war of independence
1962	Eritrea becomes a province of Ethiopia
1972–1974	Severe drought and famine
1974	Haile Selassie overthrown by military coup
1974	Insurrection breaks out in Tigre province
1975	Haile Selassie dies in prison
1977	Lt.-Col. Haile-Mariam. Mengistu becomes president and adopts Marxist policies
1977–1979	Somalia invades Ogaden
1984–1987	Further drought and famine kills thousands
1988	Ethiopia and Somalia sign peace treaty
1991	Eritrean and Tigrean forces overthrow Mengistu's regime
1992	Transitional government formed
1993	Ethiopia recognizes independence of Eritrea
1994	New constitution federates Ethiopia
1998–2000	Border war between Eritrea and Ethiopia
2002	International panel rules on border dispute

Zenawi, a former guerrilla leader, while the Eritrean People's Liberation Front (successor to the ELF) established its own regime in Asmara. Eritrea finally gained its independence in 1993: this was the last disputed colonial possession to do so in mainland Africa apart from Western Sahara.

In 1994 Ethiopia adopted a new federal constitution dividing the country into nine regions based, except for the capital and the south, on the predominant ethnic group in each region. Each region had its own assembly and was granted the right to secede following a referendum.

Relations with Eritrea remained cordial until 1998, when Eritrea and Ethiopia fought along a stretch of disputed border around the northwestern frontier town of Badme. The conflict increased in scale when Ethiopia bombed Asmara airport and Eritrea responded by bombing Mekele in northern Ethiopia.

The war continued until 2000, when, following a major Ethiopian offensive, both sides agreed to a ceasefire and peace plan brokered by the OAU, setting up a buffer zone between the two armies until the border could be demarcated on an internationally- agreed basis.

The border was agreed in 2002 with minor adjustments.

The spoils of war
This Soviet-made tank was captured by Ethiopian troops in 1977 during the Somali invasion of the Ogaden region.

The collapse of Somalia

The Republic of Somalia was created in 1960 by the merger of the former British and Italian Somalilands. Its first president, Aden Abdullah Osman, supported the creation of a Greater Somalia, including Djibouti, the (Somali-speaking) Ogaden region of Ethiopia, and part of northeast Kenya. In 1967 Osman resigned following a clan conflict and was succeeded by Abdir-Rashid Shermarke, the former prime minister. He rejected his predecessor's confrontational policies and stressed the right of self-determination for Somalis everywhere.

In the late 1960s tensions between the two (former colonial) halves of the country mounted, leading in 1969 to an army coup by Major General Muhammad Siad Barre. Shermarke was assassinated, parliament abolished, and the country, which from 1976 was a one-party state, came under Siad Barre's personal control.

Gun land

Due to Somalia's strategic importance, Siad Barre received foreign economic and military support, at first from the USSR, and later the USA. The weapons these superpowers poured into the country enabled Somalia and Ethiopia to enter into disastrous wars with each other in 1964, and again in 1977–1979, over the control of the Ogaden. It also helped to create a gun culture in the country and provided Siad Barre with the means to persecute rival clans. His hold on the country weakened as a result of food shortages caused by a severe drought in the late 1970s and the ending of US support at the end of the Cold War in the late 1980s. In January 1991 the capital, Mogadishu, fell to rebel forces and Siad Barre was deposed and fled the country.

Civil war

The rebels created political chaos. Civil conflict caused great destruction in the south while, in the north, the Somali National Movement announced its secession from Somalia and declared an independent Somaliland Republic, a secessionist state that has received no international recognition. Somalia's civil and political institutions collapsed, with none of the opposition

Abdir-Rashid Shermarke
A former prime minister and president, he was assassinated in a military coup in 1969.

politicians able to exert control. Into this power vacuum stepped at least 15 different armed factions, loosely allied to clans or sub-clans and led by regional warlords. The most powerful of these, General Muhammad Farah Aidid, did much to undermine attempts to restore order.

This breakdown of order led to severe famine and, with food deliveries from abroad interrupted by armed gangs, the UN attempted unsuccessfully to impose order between 1992 and 1994. By the turn of the century, a fragile peace existed, but the country was effectively divided in three: the armed, faction-ridden south, the northeastern area known as Puntland, and the northern Somaliland Republic.

In 2000 some hope emerged when a peace conference in Djibouti established a three-year transitional assembly to operate in Mogadishu under the presidency of Abdikassim Salad Hassan, but the new institution operated only in the south. The northeast promised to rejoin a reconstituted Somalia, but the north seemed likely to remain a separate entity.

Child soldiers
During Somalia's long civil war, arms poured in from both the former USSR and US, creating a culture of violence in which even young children were involved.

US forces in Somalia, 1992–1993
US soldiers hold back reporters and bystanders while their colleagues destroy a cache of weapons that they have found in Mogadishu, Somalia.

© DIAGRAM

Burundi, Rwanda, and genocide

Victims of genocide
A grim reminder of the aftermath when one Rwandan faction imposes its will on another.

The history of both Burundi and Rwanda since they became independent in 1962 has been one of bitter and remorseless conflict between the majority Hutu and minority Tutsi peoples in each country.

Burundi

In 1965 animosity between Hutu and Tutsi in Burundi came to a head with the assassination of the Tutsi prime minister, and an unsuccessful Hutu-led military coup. The coup was harshly repressed and most of the leaders executed. In July 1966, when King Mwambutsa IV was abroad, his son proclaimed himself king as Ntare V. Four months later, the Tutsi prime minister Michel Micombero, deposed Ntare V and declared Burundi a republic with himself as president.

In 1972 the Hutu rebelled in an attempt to overthrow Micombero and end Tutsi domination. In response the government massacred up to 200,000 Hutu. In 1976 the Tutsi Jean-Baptiste Bagaza seized power. He introduced some reforms but relations between the government and the pro-Hutu Roman Catholic Church deteriorated, causing the army to remove him from power in 1987. A Tutsi, Pierre Buyoya, replaced him and introduced conciliatory policies.

In 1993 Buyoya was defeated in the presidential election but his Hutu successor and six ministers were killed in a military coup a few months later. In 1994 the new Hutu president and the president of Rwanda were both killed when their plane was shot down by Hutu extremists, leading to Hutu–Tutsi massacres and eventual civil war.

In 1996, as the war intensified, the army seized power and reinstalled Buyoya as president. In 1998 the Oraganization for African Unity (OAU) instigated peace talks mediated by Julius Nyerere, former president of Tanzania. Following his death, former South African president Nelson Mandela took over.

In 2001 Buyoya and most Hutu and Tutsi political parties signed an agreement to set up an ethnically-balanced government and end the civil war, although conflict continued into 2002.

Rwanda

The first president of independent Rwanda was the Hutu Grégoire Kayibanda. He attempted to unite the country but, in 1963, a Tutsi force thwarted his efforts by attampting to seize power. The uprising provoked the Hutu into violent reprisals: 10,000 Tutsi were killed and 150,000 fled into neighboring countries. Kayibanda was reelected twice but, following further Hutu–Tutsi conflict and his failure to solve the country's economic problems, he was overthrown in a military coup by Juvénal Habyarimana. The new president dissolved parliament and, in 1978, made the country a one-party state.

In 1990 the Tutsi rebel Rwandan Patriotic Front (RPF), formed from the refugees in Uganda, invaded Rwanda, but were defeated with French army help. In 1991 Rwanda returned to a multi-party system but, in 1994, Habyarimana was shot down with the Burundi president in a plane crash by Hutu extremists. Hutu militia then began a campaign of genocide, killing 750,000 Tutsi.

The RPF then returned to defeat the Hutu, end the genocide, and set up a government of national unity under a moderate Hutu president. By this time, more than 2 million Hutu had fled, mainly into Zaïre (now Democratic Republic of Congo), where they helped to overthrow its government in 1997.

In 2000 Paul Kagame, effective ruler of Rwanda since 1994, became president, stressing his Rwandan rather than his Tutsi identity.

Victim of retaliation, 1972
Innocent children suffered when the Tutsi retaliated with savagery following an abortive Hutu revolt in Burundi.

Rwanda since independence	
1963	Tutsi force attempts to seize power, leading to savage Hutu reprisals
1965, 1969	President Kayibanda re-elected
1973	After renewed Hutu–Tutsi conflict, Kayibanda is overthrown; Juvénal Habyarimana becomes president
1978	Rwanda becomes a one-party state
1990	Rwandan Patriotic Front (RPF) invades country
1991	Rwanda becomes multi-party state again after second RPF invasion
1994	Habyarimana killed by Hutu extremists in a plane crash; Hutu attacks on Tutsi lead to genocide
1994	Paul Kagame and the RPF defeat Hutu forces and end genocide; government of national unity set up under moderate Hutu president
1995	War crimes trials open against those accused of genocide
2000	The moderate Tutsi Paul Kagame becomes president

© DIAGRAM

The impact of tourism

National parks and game reserves
This map shows the major national parks and game reserves in Uganda, Kenya, and Tanzania. The establishment of these protected areas curtailed many people's rights of access to vital resources. Some were even evicted from their land. Today, governments are beginning to realize the value of indigenous lifestyles that help maintain the environment and are allowing greater access to national parks and game reserves.

Since the 1970s East Africa has become a major destination for tourists attracted to its varied landscapes, wildlife, and native cultures. In the past, visitors to the region came to hunt wildlife, wiping out entire species and endangering many others. Today, the emphasis is on conservation and preservation, not destruction.

Tourism is central to the development plans of most countries in the region and has become the single most important source of foreign currency: it forms 40 percent of Kenya's earnings, and 25 percent of Tanzania's. More than 30 percent of the Seychelles' population now works in a tourist sector marketed internationally as an upmarket destination, while, since the 1990s, the political stability of Uganda has attracted increasing numbers of tourists to view its mountain gorillas, hippos, and crocodiles.

Some argue that tourism brings much-needed jobs to areas of high unemployment, but that ignores the fact that service jobs — in restaurants and hotels — are no replacement for the largely self-sufficient ways of life that many people once maintained.

Park life
During the 1940s huge tracts of land in East Africa were designated as parks, with admission reserved for

On safari (right)
Tourists are offered the chance to view wildlife in its natural habitat, and at extremely close quarters, in the areas of East Africa which have been designated as national parks, game reserves or conservation areas.

Hemingways
Named after the hunter, game fisherman, and celebrated US author, this resort is located on Turtle Bay, close to the Watamu National Maritime park in Kenya.

rangers and paying tourists. These areas were not "wilderness" but among the world's longest-inhabited areas; game concentrated in regions that, with the best grazing land and the most reliable water sources, were areas also most suitable for cattle and people.

Conflicts between the interests of indigenous peoples and wildlife conservation are well illustrated by the case of the Maasai. Between 1948 and 1988 the Maasai of Kenya were deprived of most of their dry-season pasture because it was said that people could not coexist successfully with wildlife within a park. Conservationists argued that the Maasai had endangered wildlife though hunting and overgrazing and they were thus excluded from the best of their traditional land, leading to overgrazing elsewhere. As a result, many of the parks are islands of biodiversity set amid environmental degradation.

Not surprisingly, many Maasai expelled from parks feel bitter towards tourism. Some have taken to poaching and many are actively hostile to tourists.

Sea and sand

Coastal tourism in East Africa – particularly the main resorts of Mombasa and Malindi in Kenya – has been expanding without restrictions.

Most beach hotels have been built in tourist enclaves and have resulted in local people losing their land and fishermen access to their beaches. Local women can no longer collect crabs, an important source of food; scuba diving, reef trips, and sewerage from local hotels have damaged coral reefs.

Elsewhere in East Africa coastal tourism is either in its infancy or tourist numbers are deliberately limited, so lessening environmental damage and conflict with local people.

Coups d'État in East Africa

Independence from colonial rule by various European powers proved difficult to achieve for many African nations. Yet, once independence had been achieved, various problems beset the new states.

As the maps (right) show, some nations were subject to political instability and military *coups d'état* after independence.

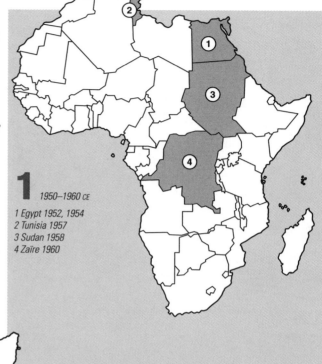

1 1950–1960 CE

1 Egypt 1952, 1954
2 Tunisia 1957
3 Sudan 1958
4 Zaïre 1960

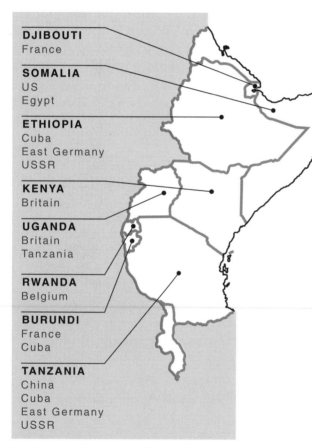

DJIBOUTI
France

SOMALIA
US
Egypt

ETHIOPIA
Cuba
East Germany
USSR

KENYA
Britain

UGANDA
Britain
Tanzania

RWANDA
Belgium

BURUNDI
France
Cuba

TANZANIA
China
Cuba
East Germany
USSR

Foreign involvement in East Africa
This map shows which foreign powers have ben involved with East African countries in the 1970s and 1980s.

Coups d'état in East Africa
Successful *coups d'état* placed these leaders in power:

Michel Micombero (left)
He deposed the King of Burundi in 1966 and made the country a republic.
Pierre Buyoya (right)
He became president of Burundi after a coup in 1996.

Haile-Mariam Mengistu (left)
He seized power from Haile Selassie I in 1974.
Juvénal Habyarimana (right)
He took power after a bloodless coup in Rwanda in 1973.

2 1961–1970 CE

1 Benin 1963, 1965, 1967, 1969
2 Congo 1963, 1968
3 Togo 1963, 1967
4 Sudan 1964, 1969
5 Algeria 1965
6 Burundi 1965, 1966
7 Central African Republic 1965
8 Zaïre 1965
9 Burkina Faso 1966
10 Ghana 1966
11 Nigeria 1966
12 Uganda 1966
13 Sierra Leone 1967, 1968
14 Mali 1968

15 Libya 1969
16 Somalia 1969
17 Lesotho 1970

3 1971–1980 CE

1 Uganda 1971, 1979
2 Benin 1972
3 Ghana 1972, 1978, 1979
4 Madagascar 1972
5 Rwanda 1973
6 Ethiopia 1974
7 Niger 1974
8 Chad 1975
9 Nigeria 1975
10 Burundi 1976
11 Congo 1977
12 Seychelles 1977
13 Comoros 1978
14 Mauritania 1978, 1980

15 Equatorial Guinea1979
16 Burkina Faso 1980
17 Central African Republic 1980
18 Guinea-Bissau 1980
19 Liberia 1980

4 1981–1990 CE

1 Central African Republic 1981
2 Ghana 1981
3 Chad 1982
4 Burkina Faso 1983, 1987
5 Nigeria 1983
6 Guinea 1984
7 Mauritania 1984
8 Sudan 1985, 198984
9 Uganda 1985
10 Lesotho 1986
11 Burundi 1987
12 Tunisia 1987
13 Somalia 1990

5 1991–2000 CE

1 Ethiopia 1991
2 Lesotho 1991, 1993
3 Mali 1991
4 Algeria 1992
5 Chad 1992
6 Sierra Leone 1992, 1997
7 Nigeria 1993
8 Gambia 1994
9 Burundi 1996
10 Niger 1996, 1999
11 Congo, Dem Rep 1997
12 Congo, Republic of 1997
13 Comoros 1999

14 Guinea-Bissau 1999
15 Ivory Coast 1999

Glossary

Allah The Muslim name for God.

annex To take over a territory through conquest or occupation.

BCE Before Common Era

CE Common Era

Christianity Religion founded by Jesus Christ at the start of the Common Era; Christians believe that Jesus was the son of God and the Messiah, or anointed one, promised to the Jews by God whose arrival marked the beginning of God's kingdom on Earth.

clan An extended family which shares an ancestor or ancestors.

Creoles Mixed-raced descendants of Africans and Europeans.

Copts The Christian people of Ethiopia, Eritrea, and Egypt; their church and ancient language are both called Coptic.

dynasty Ruling family of a country, in which power passes down, usually from father to son, through the generations.

empire A collection of different peoples and territories, often of wide extent, under the rule of one person or country.

Great Lakes The large lakes of East Africa situated in the Rift Valley as well as Lake Victoria.

Horn of Africa, the Somalia and neighboring parts of Ethiopia and Djibouti, so-called because of its shape.

Islam Religion founded by Muhammad after 622 CE with the main belief that there is only one God, and that Muhammad was his prophet; the Qur'an is the holy book of Islam.

Jesuit A member of a Roman Catholic religious order founded in 1534.

jihad Islamic holy war against non-believers.

League of Nations International organization set up in Geneva, Switzerland in 1919 after World War I to preserve international peace and settle disputes by arbitration. It collapsed after its failure to prevent territorial aggression by Germany, Japan, and Italy during the 1930s, including the Italian invasion of Ethiopia in 1935.

mandates Former German colonies in Africa and Asia administered after 1919 by, among others, Britain, France, and Belgium, on behalf of the League of Nations with the aim of eventual independence. After World War II, ultimate control of the territories was transferred to the United Nations. The trusteeship territories in East Africa, including Tanganyika and Italian Somaliland, later gained independence in the 1960s.

mercenary A soldier who fights only for pay, not to defend a country.

monarchy A system of government in which supreme power is vested in the single, hereditary figure of a king or queen.

monastery The residence of a religious community, especially of monks, living in seclusion from the rest of the world; such a system is known as monasticism.

mosque A Muslim place of worship.

Muslim A believer in Islam.

mya Million years ago.

nomads People who travel from place to place in search of pasture, food, water, or trade; the word developed from the Latin word *nomas*, which means "wandering shepherd."

Organization of African Unity (OAU) Pan-African organization established in Addis Ababa, Ethiopia, in 1963 to maintain solidarity among African states and end colonial rule on the African continent. The OAU was replaced by the African Union in 2002.

pastoralist A person who raises livestock.

protectorate A territory controlled by another, but not owned or fully colonized by it.

Protestant A Christian who belongs to a church which split from the Roman Catholic church in the 16th century; there are many different types of Protestant church.

Qur'an The holy book of Islam, often translated as the Koran.

republic A form of government in which the people or their elected representatives possess supreme power and elect their head of state.

Rift Valley Geological feature running south from Syria in the north through East Africa to Mozambique in the south.

Roman Catholic A Christian who accepts the Pope in Rome as the head of the Christian church.

sharia Islamic holy law: a body of doctrines and laws that regulate the lives of those who profess Islam.

Shi'ah The minority branch of Islam, whose followers believe that only the descendants of Muhammad's daughter, Fatima, and her husband Ali should succeed him, and that after Ali's death, God sent *imams* descended from Ali as his infallible messengers.

Sunni The majority branch of Islam, which consists of those who accept the authority of the Sunna, the code of behavior based on Muhammad's words and deeds, and who believe that the caliphs who succeeded him were his rightful successors.

trading post A port or town which foreign merchants establish in order to trade with the local people.

tributary One nation that pays tribute to another, i.e. that recognizes its authority or control.

trusteeship *See* mandates.

United Nations International organization set up in 1945 as successor to the League of Nations to maintain international peace.

Learning to read
This male student is studying Arabic at an Islamic school in Somalia. Among rural Somalis, schooling tends to be a privilege restricted to male members of the population.

© DIAGRAM

Bibliography

Buxton, David R., *The Abyssians,* London: Thames & Hudson (1970)

Camerapix, *Spectrum Guide to Tanzania,* Ashbourne (UK): Moorland Publishing Ltd. (1992)

Diagram Group, *African History On File,* New York: Facts On File (2003)

Diagram Group, *Encyclopedia of African Nations,* New York: Facts On File (2002)

Diagram Group, *Encyclopedia of African Peoples,* New York: Facts On File (2000)

Diagram Group, *Peoples of East Africa,* New York: Facts On File (1997)

Diagram Group, *Religions On File,* New York: Facts On File (1990)

Diagram Group, *Timelines On File, 4 vols.* New York: Facts On File (2000)

Laughlin, Charles, D., and Allgeier, Elizabeth R., *An Ethnography of the So of Northeastern Uganda.* 2 vols. New Haven, Conn.:Human Relations Area Files (1979)

Kaplan, Steven, *The Beta Israel: Falasha in Ethiopia,* New York: New York University Press (1992)

Kobishchanov, Youri M., *Axum,* University Park, Pa.: Pennsylvania State University Press (1979)

Lambert, David and the Diagram Group, *The Field Guide to Early Man,* New York: Facts On File (1987)

Leakey, Richard, *The Origin of Humankind,* New York: Basic Books (1994)

Mazrui, A., *The African Condition,* Oxford (UK): Heinemann (1986)

Mukherjee, R., *Uganda: an Historical Accident?,* Trenton, N.J.: Africa World Press (1985)

Nyaka Tura, J., *An Anatomy of an African Kingdom: History of Bunyoro-Kitara,* New York: Anchor Press (1973)

Odhiambo, A., Ouso, T., and Williams, J.*A., History of East Africa,* Harlow (UK): Longman Group (1977)

Ogot, Bertwell, *Zamani: a Survey of East African History,* Nairobi, Kenya: East African Publishing House (1974)

Parfitt, Tudor, *Operation Moses: the Story of the Exodus of the Falasha Jews from Ethiopia,* New York: Stein & Day (1985)

Ray, B. C., *Myth, Ritual and Kingship in Buganda,* New York: Oxford University Press (1991)

Roy, C.D., *Art and Life in Africa,* Iowa, IA.: University of Iowa Museum of Art (1992)

Shelemay, K., *Music, Ritual and Falasha History,* East Lansing, Mi.: Michigan State University (1986)

Soyinka, W., *Myth, Literature and the African World,* Cambridge (UK): Cambridge University Press (1990)

Timberlake, Lloyd., *Africa in Crisis,* London: Earthscan (1988)

Turle, G., *The Art of the Maasai,* New York: Alfred A. Knopf (1992)

Were, G. S., and Wilson, D. A., *East Africa Through a Thousand Years,* London: Evans (1985)

Wills, A.J., *The Story of Africa,* New York: Africana (1972)

Index

Index

Index

Shermarke, Abdar-Rashid 98
slavery and the slave trade
49, 62, 67–70, 73, 76, 82
Solomon, King 30, 33
Somalia and the Somalis 8,
10, 17, 42–4, 84, 89, 92,
98–9
Speke, John Hanning 52
Stanley, Henry Morton 67
Sudan 41; *see also* Nubia
Susenyos, Seltan Sagad 38,
40
Swahili people 46–7, 68, 72

T

Taitu, Queen of Ethiopia 82–3
Tanganyika 79–80, 88
Tanzania 8, 88, 93–4, 102
Tewodros II of Ethiopia 74
Tigre 75, 96–7
tools, ancient 24

Toro 55
tourism 102–3
trade 49, 62, 67, 70, 72–3,
93, 107; *see also* Indian
Ocean trade
Ts'akha Maryam 31
Tunisia 70
Tutsi people 56–7, 89, 92,
100–1

U

Uganda 8, 81, 88, 92, 94–5,
102
Uganda Railway *see* East
Africa Railway
United Nations 85, 88–9,
98–9, 107
United States 98
Unyamwezi 62
Urundi 56–7, 79, 89;

W

World War I 78–9, 83
World War II 86–7

Y

Yao people 72–3
Yekuno Amlak 33
Yohannes IV of Ethiopia 32,
74

Z

Zabid 32
Zagwe dynasty 32–3, 36, 40
Zaire 101
Zanzibar 47, 49–51, 63,
66–70, 81, 88
Zauditu, Empress of Ethiopia
83–4
Zenawi, Meles 97